Landfall Walks Books No. 12

BOB ACTON

A VIEW FROM TRENCROM

The village pump at Angarrack (Walk 6)

Round Walks near Hayle, St Ives and Penzance

First published 1992 by
LANDFALL PUBLICATIONS
Landfall, Penpol, Devoran, Truro, Cornwall TR3 6NW
Telephone Truro (0872) 862581

A CIP catalogue record for this book is available from the British Library.

ISBN 1 873443 05 6

IMPORTANT NOTE

I have done my best to ensure that all the recommended routes are on public rights of way, with a few unavoidable exceptions mentioned in the text, and that they are all unobstructed. If you come across unexpected difficulties (new fences, changed field-boundaries, rotted footbridges, waist-deep mud ....) please be patient, take the nearest practicable alternative route, and if possible let me know about the problem so that I can refer to it in any future edition of this book. Please help farmers and other landowners by leaving all gates as you found them, and by keeping dogs on a lead when there are livestock nearby.

USING THE BOOK

The boxed note at the start of each walk description is intended to be read before you set out; sometimes it would be useful to make preparations a day or two in advance in order to get the most out of the walk. A star (*) indicates that there is a boxed note on this point - usually but not always on the same page. The directions attempt to be very exact and explicit, but the maps are only rough sketches, so I'd strongly recommend taking with you the relevant Ordnance Survey maps. Landranger 203 (Land's End) covers all the routes. Best of all for walkers is the Pathfinder series; the sheets named "Camborne (South) and Hayle", "Helston and Prussia Cove" and "St Ives and Penzance (North)" are the relevant ones.

Typesetting, maps and illustrations by Bob Acton unless otherwise stated

Printed by the Troutbeck Press
and bound by R. Booth Ltd., Antron Hill, Mabe, Penryn, Cornwall

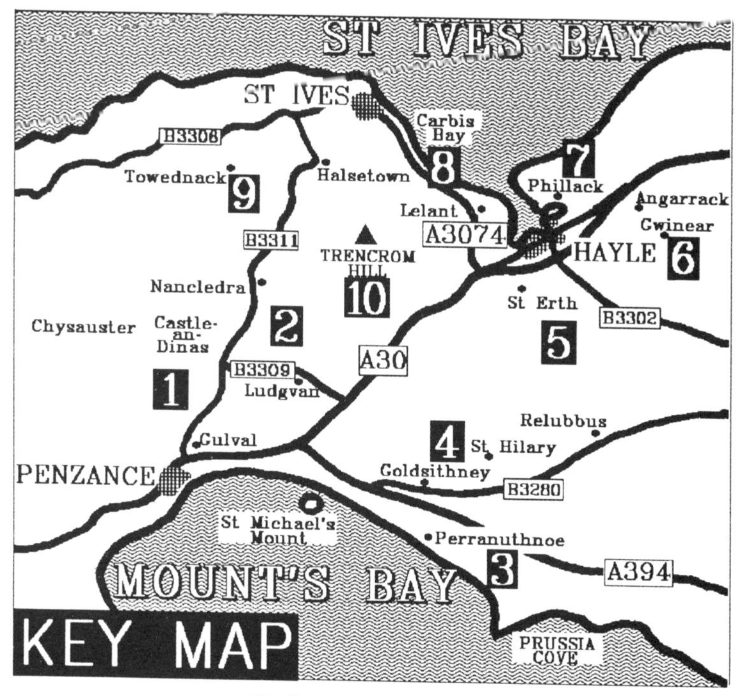

CONTENTS

FRONT COVER: "On Trencrom" (1990) by Jennifer Jenkins
BACK COVER: "Summer Wind - St Michael's Mount" (1991) by Derek Jenkins
Both are photographs of original pastel paintings.

ACKNOWLEDGEMENTS

For the Hayle walkabout I am indebted to Bill Newby, Hon. Secretary of the Trevithick Society, who fired my interest in Hayle first at a lecture and then by leading a guided tour. He has also kindly checked through the texts of the Hayle, Phillack and Lelant walks for me, and supplied photographs. A visit to Wheal Sisters organised by the Trevithick Society also proved valuable to me in researching this book, and that too was led partially by Mr Newby, but principally by Kenneth Brown. Once again I have called on Mr Brown's encyclopedic knowledge of Cornish mining - especially matters related to engines - to help me to avoid factual errors. He recently gave me a graphic account of what has now become a rather frequent occurrence: a heavy thud on the doormat disturbs the early-morning tranquillity of Bell Lake, and he knows Bob Acton's been working on another book. No doubt the prospect of wading through yet one more fat sheaf of computer print-outs blights the day for him, but within a few weeks he unfailingly returns them, liberally annotated with corrections and comments as interesting as they are meticulous. A third person who has gone to considerable trouble to help me with this book is Graham Thorne, who despite living in remotest Essex is another Trevithick Society member, with a special interest in Cornish railways. A faithful collector of Landfall Walks Books, he has fed me with a steady stream of interesting "snippets" over the past two or three years, and recently with a wealth of very useful material, mainly about Hayle, the Hayle railway and the St Ives branch line. The list of others who have helped is long, so I hope they will forgive me for mentioning them only briefly: Mr W. T. (Bill) Tregenza of the Gwinear and District Footpaths and Bridleways Association, for suggesting attractive walks in his parish and supplying information on local history; Mr C. J. Rogers of Camborne for checking through the St Hilary / Goldsithney walk and making valuable contributions; Father Francis Sutcliffe, now Rector of Ilchester, for help with the history of Acton Castle; Mr Chris Massie of the Poldice Valley Trust for information about the recent history of Hayle; Mr Donald Bray for permission to use an extract from his poem about Angarrack; and the many people who spent time chatting with my wife and me about their villages, houses or districts, notably Ms Rosemary Balmer at Lelant, Mr Mike Hunt at Angarrack, Ms Doris Harry at Tredrea (St Erth), Miss Thelma Hocking at Gulval, Mr Barry Rodda at Rosemorran Farm, Mrs J. Savill at Lelant Downs Post Office, and Mr Simon Hall at the Star Inn, St Erth. I should also like to thank Mrs E. B. Williams of the Copperhouse Book Centre, who has uncomplainingly stocked my earlier books, however few copies of them she expected to sell, and has given me very encouraging support in my efforts to produce this one. As usual, I must ask anyone else who deserved thanks but has been overlooked here to forgive my bad memory.

INTRODUCTION

I am seriously thinking of giving up writing introductions. After all, I don't suppose anyone actually reads them, with the exception of newspaper reviewers whose deadline for copy was yesterday and who therefore haven't got time to wade through any of the actual accounts of the walks and the places en route. (The introduction to *Around St Austell,* for example, produced the arresting headline, **AUTHOR ADMITS TO BIG MISTAKE**, because I had started by saying that until researching the book I had not expected to enjoy walking in that area.) On the other hand, I suppose I should learn from the example of medieval craftsmen who laboured devotedly to produce beautiful carvings destined to be fixed to the roofs of cathedrals where no eye other than God's would ever see them ..... No, the point I wanted to make is that it becomes increasingly difficult to think of variations on the basic message: Here is another fascinating area, full of beauty and variety. If you have never explored it, I envy you the enjoyment you have in store; and if you already know it, I hope that a few of the things I have discovered with the help of many other people will be new to you, and give you an incentive to return to your old haunts. The subject of this book is Cornwall's narrow neck, and most of the routes include uplands giving views of both coasts as well as many miles inland, especially to the east. Every walk except the last one features an ancient parish church, and of course there is much to interest the archaeologist, whether he or she is of the "ancient" or "industrial" variety.

A special feature of this book is the inclusion of a "town trail". Here comes another admission of a big mistake. In the days when the A30 ran through the middle of Hayle I never stopped the car there unless traffic jams forced me to, and was always pleased to leave a place that looked as ugly as it was boring. Now I realise that it is a uniquely important monument to Cornwall's industrial history. Despite so much wanton destruction during the past few years, it still retains more evidence of its great days in the 18th and 19th centuries than do most of the industrial towns of the midlands and the north. Walk 7 in this book occupies more pages than any other I have written for earlier publications, despite the fact that I was conscious of omitting dozens of details which seemed interesting and important. "Boring" Hayle certainly isn't, and I can now no longer see it as ugly, because the neglect which makes parts of it so tatty is also the reason why so much of interest is still there. Besides, the natural setting is magnificent, there are some fine buildings, and places such as The Plantation and the recently restored Ropewalk and Hammermill area are attractive by any standards.

For me, then, the "discovery" of Hayle was one of the outstanding pleasures of working on this book, but what of all the delightful and historic villages in this area (St Erth, Gulval, Ludgvan, St Hilary, Angarrack .....), the splendid scenery on both coasts, the lonely granite moors and the pretty sheltered valleys? For all those and more, "Enquire Within".

Bob Acton

WALK 1

GULVAL AND CASTLE-AN-DINAS, with a possible extension to CHYSAUSTER ANCIENT VILLAGE

A little over 6 miles, or about 7.5 including Chysauster.

Here is a walk with breathtaking views almost all the way, so try to choose a clear day for it. At the highest point, the site of a prehistoric hill fort, a panorama embracing both coasts opens up; and most of the return half of the walk offers wonderful views of Mount's Bay. Gulval Church is a beautiful building surrounded by a flower-filled and lovingly tended churchyard, itself encircled by a very harmonious group of late-Victorian granite houses. The countryside of the first and last parts of the walk is rolling, fertile-looking farmland; in February, when we did this walk on a gloriously sunny day, much of it was devoted to vast, creamy broccoli and masses of daffodils, together with some other flower-crops such as anemones. The lower slopes of the parish have long been known for growing two crops of potatoes per year, with the aid of seaweed fertiliser and the marine climate; the practice nowadays is to assist the early crop with acres of polythene which look from a distance like lakes set at crazy angles. Unfortunately, high winds tend to rip up the plastic and deposit tatty streamers of it in the trees and hedges. The higher ground surrounding Castle-an-Dinas is much more bare and bleak - granite moorland, in fact, and the granite is being quarried on a large scale on the southern slopes of the hill. If you want to enjoy peace and quiet at Castle-an-Dinas, go on a Sunday, when the quarry is less likely to be working. Blasting takes place at the quarry occasionally (usually only about once a week, at about midday or 4 pm), and if you chanced to be there when that was happening you would have to wait about twenty minutes before passing along the road nearest to the pit. Noise can be a bit of a problem at Gulval, too: the main roads are close, but more intrusive can be the racket produced by helicopters preparing for the flight to Scilly. Between the two, however, all is usually peaceful. There are many attractive buildings along the way: old farmhouses and barns, thatched cottages, and a late-18th-century tower on the hilltop. The higher region is full of evidence of ancient habitation, and a short diversion would enable you to visit one of the best-preserved ancient villages in Britain. The only pub and shop on the route are at Gulval; we set off from there about 10 am, took a picnic with us and ate it at Rogers' Tower, which would have provided shelter if we had needed it. After the downhill walk back to Gulval we were much too early for evening opening-time at the Coldstreamer Inn, but a local told us it's a very friendly pub and serves good food. Nearly half a mile of the route is along a B-road. There are many stiles to cross on this walk, a few of them quite awkward, and some gates to climb; you will also need good boots to cope with stony ground and some deep mud. One or two patches looked as if they might get rather overgrown in the summer or autumn. It's a splendid walk, though, and you mustn't let such trivial difficulties put you off.

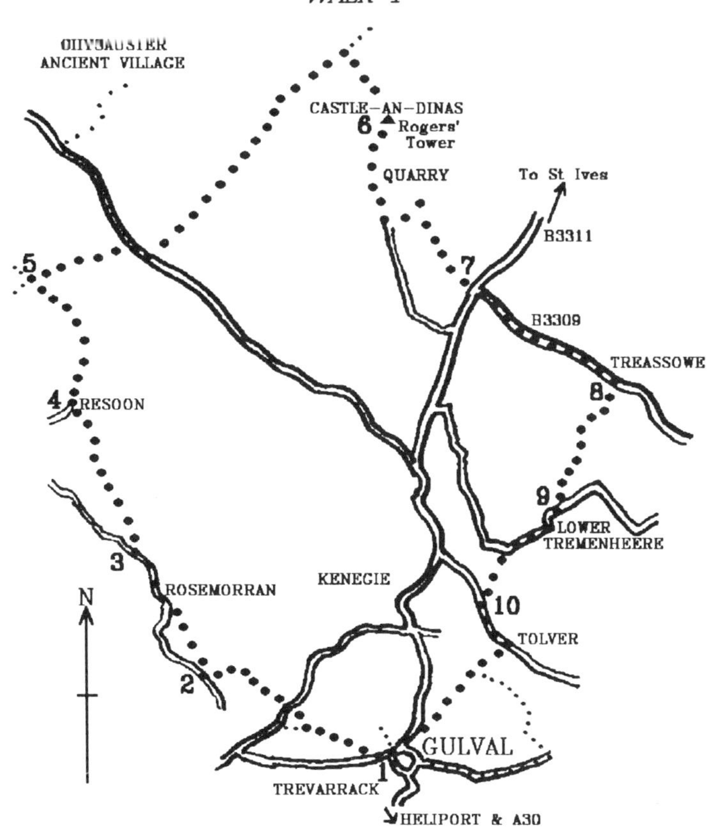

Directions are given from Gulval Church, which is close to the heliport on the north side of the A30 just east of Penzance. If you take the turning for the heliport at the roundabout west of Longrock, you will find Gulval signposted to the right, close to the heliport entrance. Roadside parking is usually available near the church, but may be hard to find during services.

1 From the main gate into the churchyard at Gulval (*), walk round past the pub and turn left. Take the signed footpath on the right beside Trevean Farmhouse. At first it is narrow and runs between hedges, but then it continues ahead across a field. Already there is a fine view to the left of the sea and Penzance, and a short climb up the little outcrop on the right gives you a nice picture of the church tower with St Michael's Mount beyond. Where the tracks divide, continue ahead. Steps take you down to a minor road close to a cottage which was being re-thatched when we were there. Cross the road and continue on the track ahead, but instead of going straight on turn left as soon as you have passed the old barn, walking downhill towards a stream. Earth-moving in this area had created something of a morass in February, but soon the tractor-track resumed and brought us down to a footbridge. Cross that and go straight on, uphill; yellow arrows provide confirmation that you're still on the right course. A few steps up bring you to a small gate; beyond that, continue ahead with the hedge on your right.

GULVAL

In 1991 the Cornwall Federation of Women's Institutes published *The Cornwall Village Book.* The village shown on the cover was Gulval, and in several ways it was a very apt choice: in the background is St Michael's Mount, a scene which symbolises Cornwall for many people; also prominent is a typical Cornish medieval church, its castellated tower peeping out from among tall trees; and no less typical in their way are the factory chimney down near the shore and the building closest to the camera, a corrugated-iron shed. Especially characteristic of this district is the field of broccoli in which the photographer was standing. Apart from that shed, however, the buildings that cluster around the church are wholly *un*typical of Cornish "churchtowns". It is now almost exactly a century since all the old cottages at Gulval were pulled down and replaced by a "model village" of sturdy Victorian granite houses. Many if not all of the ones near the church have large barns behind them, which were built just before the cottages were demolished, to provide temporary accommodation during the rebuild. A few moments wandering around Gulval are enough to reveal the name behind this scheme: Bolitho. The pub, for example, which bears a plaque saying that the Gulval Institute was erected by Richard Foster Bolitho of Ponsandane in 1895, was originally "Ye Olde Inn" but was renamed "The Coldstreamer" in tribute to a Bolitho who was killed while serving with the Coldstream Guards in World War II. The Bolitho family amassed a large fortune in the 18th and 19th centuries, operating the largest tin-smelting works in Cornwall at Chyandour (about half a mile south-west of the church), where they also ran a tannery and a bank. Among the mansions they built for themselves were Trengwainton, now famous for its National Trust garden, and Ponsandane, close to the smelter but not so close as to be plagued by its "black murky smoke all day and all night" (see Peter Laws: *The Industries of Penzance).* In early times the parish was called Lanisley or Lanestly, the name of the chief manor; "Gulval" refers to the church's patron saint, about whom nothing certain is known. The church is usually locked, but if you do get the chance to look inside notice the memorial to the Harris family of Kenegie (see the note about Castle-an-Dinas); it is at the east end of the south aisle. The list of vicars, displayed beside the south entrance, is worth study: for example, contrast the very short incumbency of Sir Henry Osberne (1349 was the year of the Black Death), with the staying powers of William Wriothesley Wingfield, whose 73 years as Vicar must challenge for a place in the record books. The chancel ceiling was painted to mark his 50th year in office; a floor plaque in his memory is now hidden by the carpet. If you have to stay outside, you can at least enjoy the well-planted churchyard and admire the 15th-century tower. The clock is another memorial to Mr Wingfield. Beside the south door is some stone tracery from the old east window, replaced during the Victorian restoration, and two parts of an old "preaching cross" (described by Rev. F.W.Warnes in his 1981 church guide as Saxon), which were discovered in the east wall at that time. Nothing is left now of the once-famous Gulval Holy Well, which is said to have been just south of the west end of the church.The shop and most of the newer houses of Gulval are south-west of the church at Trevarrack.

2 At the gate, where there is a stone cattle-grid, turn right on the surfaced road, and take the signed path ahead, starting on the left side of the gate marked Rosemorran. Walk with the trees and hedge on your right at first, then across the field to Rosemorran, with its lonely palm tree overlooking the splendid view. Cross the stile and continue ahead on the road. (There is a beautiful old cross at Rosemorran; to see it you need to turn right at the farm entrance and seek permission at the farm if possible to walk just past a black-painted outbuilding and a holiday cottage; the cross is on the left there. About six years ago, three gold bracelets were found, close to the cross; they have been pronounced by authorities at the British Museum to be 3,000 years old.) The road takes you past the intriguing, long, ecclesiastical-looking, thatched Rosemorran House, with a small cross over its entrance. Mr Barry Rodda, the owner, tells me that there was a monastery here in the 14th century, and that the large main room or hall retains its Gothic window. Rosemorran is said to be haunted by the ghost of a monk, but Mr Rodda hasn't yet encountered him. Gerald Priestland has a little to say about the house in *West of Hayle River;* and according to the W.I. book (see the note on Gulval), "an old story said that at midnight the two stone pillars at the bottom of the park changed places!" The name refers to moorland (Cornish *ros);* "morran" is said by Polsue to be from *moyr,* blackberries, which would probably be very apt, even if the etymology is false. On the skyline to the left is the lonely engine-house of Ding Dong Mine (*), and Rogers' Tower is visible on the right close to the large quarry.

DING DONG MINE

This is one of the most spectacularly situated mines in Cornwall, and reputedly one of the oldest. Dines mentions the claim that some of its lodes were discovered "in distant, possibly in pre-historic, times," and the legend that Jesus Christ visited Cornwall sometimes includes Ding Dong Mine on the itinerary. Its main active period, though, began in 1814. The conspicuous engine house, on Greenburrow Shaft, was built in 1865 for a 40-inch pumping engine; nearby are the ruins of the whim and stamps houses. The surface remains of the mine may look romantic now in their splendid isolation, but the harsh realities of its working days are conveyed in Cyril Noall's *Cornish Mine Disasters:* he tells of men being badly scalded by a methane explosion underground caused by rotting timbers (1868), and recounts two horrific accidents to children (1867 and 1873). The mine, which produced tin, closed in 1878 or 1880; unsuccessful attempts to re-work it were made in 1912 and 1928. Its name (which it shares with a mine near Gunnislake on the Devon-Cornwall border) has, as far as I know, not been explained. As well as the two Ding Dong mines there was a Wheal Ding near Lanivet and Ting Tang Mine near St Day. Perhaps the intention was to suggest a triumphant peal of bells: many mines were blessed with optimistic names that sound ironic or melancholy now: Prosper, Good Speed, Fortune, Joy, Triumph, Glory..... Gerald Priestland, in *West of Hayle River,* says "There really is a Ding Dong bell, and you can see it inside the church at Madron." I'm intending to get along there to find out what he means.

3 Go through the gate on the right, near a footpath sign. (Take care in opening the gate: it's liable to fall down!) We walked round the field-edge on the left because the field had been planted, but the actual path cuts off the corner and then runs a short way beside the hedge to a granite stile. Cross that and walk to the far right-hand corner of the next field, where there is another stile. Go on in the same direction, through a gate, over the next stile, then almost straight on - very slightly right - to yet another stile. The field beyond that was planted and there was no sign of the path, which in fact goes across the middle of it, curving slightly left to pass through a small stile and reach the track between the farm buildings and the cottage (Resoon, "moor-down").

4 Turn right, passing the cottage, and then keep to the rather muddy main tractor-track leading down into the valley. Where the track ends, keep by the hedge on your left, and at the bottom take the path going left, which winds among bramble-patches at first, with a barbed wire fence and the Rosemorran Stream on your right. Soon the path goes a little further left to a stone stile beside a small gate. Keep by the field edge after that, and go through the rather rickety wooden gate. Ignore the path going right: keep on the main one to the left of the stream. One unavoidable patch was extremely muddy in February - luckily it was only a few feet across. After a long, grassy field, another stile beside a gate brings you to a made-up road.

CHYSAUSTER

This famous archaeological site has been very fully described in numerous publications, including a guide available at the entrance kiosk, so I will content myself with giving the barest facts - or theories - about it. The remains of a village street and nine courtyard houses have been discovered, two of which are almost complete apart from roofs. The village was probably inhabited by a farming community, possibly with some tin-streamers among them, from about 100 BC to 300 AD, and is likely to have relied on protection from the nearby hill fort. On the north-east side of the settlement was (until much of it was destroyed in 1984) an ancient field system, and to the south are the ruins of a fogou or possibly two. (Fogous are passages, usually lined and roofed with stone, found at many ancient sites west of Falmouth; archaeologists disagree about their purpose, but they are usually thought to have been food stores.)

5 Turn right on that. Up on the left now you can get a glimpse of Chysauster - or at least of the custodian's hut at the entrance. At the road, *turn left if you want to extend the walk to Chysauster (*). The path to it is signposted to the right after about a quarter of a mile. Return the same way.* Turn right to continue to Castle-an-Dinas. After a short distance, cross the wooden stile on the left, beside a holly tree. The rough path leads uphill, becoming the bed of a small stream for about a hundred yards. There is a wooden stile to cross near the top of the hill, and then as you approach the quarry tips cross another wooden stile on the right of a gate, and continue on the track ahead. When you reach the wide quarry road, continue almost straight ahead on the signed path. This now takes you over the brow of the hill and reveals at least a hint of a view of the north coast. Watch, now, for a narrow but distinct footpath on the right. Where it passes through the hedge there are rusty posts on each side; it then runs uphill, and goes to the left of a wooden post as it approaches the top of the hill. At this point it runs through the two ditches and ramparts of Castle-an-Dinas (*); soon you reach the trig. point stone and Rogers' Tower.

6 When you're ready for the return trip, take the path which heads south-west, roughly towards the prominent tower of Penzance Church (not towards the Mount). This path will bring you back to the main quarry road close to the line of tall gravel-heaps; turn left on that. It runs quite close to the main quarry pit, past a large sand-tip, and brings you to the office hut at the main entrance to the quarry. (Incidentally, the OS maps appear to indicate a public footpath running a little to the west of the quarry road, but there seems to be no sign of it on the ground now. The quarry official we spoke to confirmed that there is no objection to walkers using the road, although of course great care is needed in an area where heavy vehicles are often on the move, and the route has to be closed briefly at times of blasting.) At the quarry office turn left past the larger wooden building, where there is a public footpath sign. The path - actually a bridleway, so you must expect some soggy patches - soon curves left, running beneath a tall "landscaped" spoil heap (on your left); later there is a right bend, and now you are walking towards the Mount.

CASTLE-AN-DINAS

There is another, even larger, Iron Age hill fort with the same name, south of St Columb Major. Although the name could be translated as "Castle Castle", other possible interpretations are "settlement at the fort" or "fort on the tor". There were originally at least four concentric lines of defence, although the outermost rampart seems to have been built only on the north-west side; the two nearest the centre were drystone walls. Dr Borlase in the 18th century and Charles Henderson early in the 20th both found the remains of several huts, but little if anything of them survives now. Castle-an-Dinas has, as Craig Weatherhill puts it in *Belerion*, "suffered terribly over the centuries at the hands of stone-robbers" (see the comment about Rogers' Tower at the end of this note, for example), and the constant noise of machinery at the quarry on working days detracts from the sort of "atmosphere" that makes it easy to commune with the distant past and fully enjoy the glorious scenery. But it remains an impressive and memorable place, and it's no surprise that a well-known ghost-story is associated with it. This concerns Wild Harris, one of several ghosts of the Harris family of Kenegie, an old manor house near Rosemorran. The ghosts were exorcised by Parson Polkinghorn of St Ives, and Wild Harris was condemned to count the grass blades within the inner enclosure at Castle-an-Dinas. His soul was denied rest until he was able to arrive at the same total nine times in succession. The tower built in a gap on the south-eastern side of the earthwork was erected in 1798 by the Rogers family of Treassowe (see the later note). It's a useful and some would say attractive landmark, but has earned the condemnation of archaeologists because it appears to be built of stones taken from the inner ramparts.

7 Cross the B3311 with care and continue ahead on the B3309. This road is usually less busy, but the traffic can be fast. Walking on the right, preferably on the verge where possible, is not only safer but also gives you the best views of the Mount. After the slight left bend the view ahead is of Tregonning Hill with Godolphin Hill on its left and Ludgvan Church down to the right.

8 As you reach the farm buildings at Treassowe (*), several of them now converted into holiday cottages, take the signed public footpath which starts at a stile on the right. The path crosses the field to a stile on the left side of a gate; beyond that, walk with the hedge on your right, go through the gateway and continue along a farm track, still with the hedge on the right. Don't go through the next gap, but keep left of the hedge curving left. Cross the stone stile at the corner. You may have to duck under low branches as you cross what looks like an old lane. Continue ahead over a low wall and a second stile, then go diagonally left over a field to a stile near a tall footpath sign.

9 Turn right on the minor road. Soon you pass Lower Tremenheere, another farm which has taken advantage of its wonderful seaward views to attract

TREASSOWE

Treassowe Manor was the site of a medieval chapel; according to Charles Henderson, an arch apparently dating from the 14th or 15th century now forms the back entrance of the farmhouse. There are also some mullioned windows, the head of an old granite cross and what the Ludgvan Church Guide calls "a curious niche" in the wall of a ruined room which could have been the chapel. Treassowe was the home of the Rogers family, one of whom had the tower of that name erected at Castle-an-Dinas; Henderson, writing during the period 1910-24, says, "The old mansion of the Rogers family is now in ruins and dates from the 17th century." It seems they had trouble with ghosts: "About the year 1761 a pinnacle was thrown down, by lightning, from the tower of the church at Ludgvan. The effect was then universally imputed to the vengeance of a perturbed spirit, exorcised from Treassow, and passing eastward, towards the usual place of banishment - THE RED SEA." (From Robert Hunt's *Popular Romances of the West of England)* Apparently Treassowe had almost as much bother with ghosts as nearby Kenegie: the Ludgvan Church guidebook mentions that Rev. John Stephens, Rector of Ludgvan 1791-1834, "was called upon to exorcise a spirit which was troubling the inhabitants of Treassowe Manor".

holiday visitors. The name shows that a standing stone ("menhir") was located nearby - probably closer to Higher Tremeneer, a little to the north; that has vanished now, as has Lower Tremenheere Mill. Where the road bends right at a cottage named (in February 1992) Hilly Field, go down on the left, where there is a footpath sign. Beyond the stile the path doubles as the bed of a streamlet until you come down to the bridge over the main stream. A very pretty spot here; it looks as though there's a good crop of "white bluebells" or ramsons later in the season. After the old wooden gate, walk by the hedge on the right, through a gap and diagonally left across the next field, heading towards Penzance church. After the next stile continue in the same line to a low stile at the field corner, where there is a footpath sign.

10 Turn left on the road, and just as you reach Tolver farm take the path on the right, immediately after you have passed the first small farm building. Cross the wooden stile (or what is left of it: it was little more than a low fence when we were there), and go to the wooden gate to your left. This has to be climbed, a task not made easier by some bits of barbed wire and other obstructions. Having negotiated that, walk beside the hedge on your right and cross the wooden stile ahead, followed immediately by two stone stiles. *(Between them is an old lane or sunken path, marked as a right of way but now thoroughly overgrown. Luckily, the direct way back to Gulval is straight on, and although this path is not indicated as a right of way on the maps it is clearly in frequent use, and includes a succession of well-maintained stiles. The local farmer we spoke to implied that the "official" path, going left, may be cleared before long, and perhaps if and when that happens objections may be made to the use of the direct path, so I have shown the alternative route on the map. It would add about half a mile to the walk.)*

As things stand, then, continue straight ahead. At the second stile, Gulval Church comes into view. Go round the left edge of the next field, then through a narrow gap, down a few steps and along a grassy lane which looked as if it might get rather overgrown at times. Turn left at the road, and soon you are back at the church.

Before the rebuilding of Gulval: a cottage beside the churchyard about a hundred years ago.

WALK 2

LUDGVAN, CRIPPLESEASE AND NANCLEDRA

About 7.5 miles. Shorter routes (about 3 and 5.5 miles) are also given.

This splendidly varied walk makes an ideal all-day ramble. If you base the walk on Ludgvan, the Engine Inn at Cripplesease would make a good lunch-stop unless you prefer to take a picnic; equally, you could park at Nancledra and call at the White Hart beside the church at Ludgvan for lunch. The countryside hereabouts is mostly high downland with wonderful views, crisscrossed by wooded or bracken-filled valleys with busy streams and old watermills now, sadly, very un-busy. Both Ludgvan and Nancledra are attractive, granite-built villages; there are many old cottages and farm buildings along the way - quite a lot of them look recently restored as holiday accommodation; and there is a great deal on this route to interest those who like to learn about Cornwall's old mines. It's those views I remember most vividly, though: St Michael's Mount and the fine tower of Ludgvan church silhouetted against the shimmering sea; Castle-an-Dinas, with a great quarry gouged out of the hillside below it; and especially one spot among ruined mine buildings just south of Cripplesease from which we could see not only the nearby Trencrom and Trink Hill, but Tregonning Hill, Godolphin Hill and even Carn Brea. The rewards of such a walk are, I hope you'll agree, ample compensation for having to cope with several very muddy and/or rather overgrown stretches of path, some ploughed-and-planted fields to cross, plus a good many awkward stiles and gates that need climbing. I'd certainly recommend you to take stout, waterproof boots and a stick, and not to wear shorts unless you have well-hardened legs. Apart from the pubs and The Wink at Cripplesease, which advertises cream teas, the only place we noticed where you might be able to get provisions was the post office in Nancledra. There are public toilets near that. A useful companion on the southern part of this walk, especially if natural history interests you, would be Des Hannigan's "Wildlife Walkabouts: Land's End Peninsula, Cornwall" (Wayside Books, 1986).

LUDGVAN AND ITS CHURCH

There seems to be no foundation for the belief that the village takes its name from an ancient Irish missionary called Ludewon, Lewdegran or something similar: Oliver Padel suggests "place of ashes", possibly a reference to a burial-site. He also gives the pronunciation of the name as "Ludjan" or "Lidjan"; this is supported in a book I have dated 1810, but not by the lady who showed my wife and me around the church: she pronounced the name as written. On sale in the church is an unusually well-produced and interesting guide which includes notes about 21 of the rectors between 1299 and the present day. From this can be culled a good deal about the history of the area: for example, the parish population nearly doubled during the incumbency of John Stephens (1791-1834) because of the growth of mining, and his successor was moved by the increasing popularity of inns and beer-shops to write a letter addressed to "Tipplers, Landlords and Constables". Two rectors who achieved celebrity were William Borlase (1695-1772, rector from 1722), the leading historian of Cornwall of his time, and Arthur Townshend Boscawen (1862-1939, rector from 1893), who was an authority on flora and horticulture. Two other names often mentioned in connection with Ludgvan are William Oliver (1695-1764), baptised here, a leading physician but best-remembered now for his "Bath Oliver Biscuits"; and Humphry Davy, whose parents are buried in the church. (Humphry himself was born in Penzance, but only because his mother was on a shopping expedition there at the time - so, at least, we were assured by the lady mentioned earlier.) Of the Norman church little besides the font has survived; the chancel dates from the early 14th century, and the north aisle and the magnificent tower - built of the attractive sparkling Ludgvan Granite used to face many of the grander houses in Penzance - from the 15th. Major alterations and restorations took place in 1840, 1888 and 1912-13. During the last of those an important pewter crucifix was discovered, attributed to the 12th century; it is now in the British Museum. A fresco of St Christopher dating from 1740 was discovered on the wall around the now blocked north door during Borlase's time; a reduced copy of his drawing of it is displayed in the church, and the guide book includes his detailed description. It seems to have been a protest by the priest against the witholding of tithes due to him. Borlase decided that "such Fooleries" deserved no place in a church, and destroyed it. Other details of interest include a grave-marker probably dating from the 7th century and three old crosses, all in the churchyard, the shaft of another old cross used as a step inside the tower, and a small granite carving found in the rectory garden wall and now above the south porch. It seems to portray a monk carrying a spade and a cross - sometimes identified as the mythical St Lewdegran, who is still commemorated on the parish feast day (25 January) despite the re-dedication of the church to St Paul in 1336. One of the ancient legends about Ludgvan is that its patron saint created a holy well whose waters protected anyone baptised in them from hanging; the well has gone now, along with the forests in which the last wolf in Britain is said to have lived - "a gigantic specimen" which was finally captured at Rospeith Farm, Ludgvan, after killing a child.

There is a convenient area for parking beside Ludgvan church (*). Ludgvan is signposted from the A30 just south of Crowlas. If you prefer to start and end the walk at Nancledra (point 10 in the directions), there is room for a few cars to park near the post office, on the left side of the road as you drive south from St Ives on the B3311.

1 Leave the churchyard at Ludgvan via the rusty wrought-iron gate on the north side and turn right on a rough, probably muddy track. The hill on the skyline to the left is crowned by the folly called Rogers' Tower (1798), and also, less obviously, by the Iron Age hill fort known as Castle-an-Dinas. Beyond a stile you are on a rather twisty path. Ignore the first left fork but take the second, immediately beyond it, then fork right, downhill. After ducking under a couple of fallen trees you come down to a sturdy stone footbridge over a pretty stream. Continue along the path that runs almost straight ahead, over a wooden stile (the top bar lifts) and uphill. A stile beside a gate close to cottages brings you to a road; cross that and go on in the same direction past more cottages. Keep to the main track till you come to a pair of stiles. Cross the one on the left. The path takes you down to another well-made footbridge, then up, beside the hedge on your left. Notice the view of the Mount now - and soon it gets even better.

2 At the minor road go left, among the restored cottages at Nanceddan, climb the steepish stone stile and walk beside the hedge on the right. After another high stile go on in the same direction across the next field to the rather tumbledown stile on the left side of a lonely house with a superb view.

3 Turn left on the road and fork right by the "Ford" sign. This little road runs above a deep valley with big granite boulders strewn about among the gorse and bracken on its sides. The stream is one of several in Cornwall called the Red River (two others flow into the sea at Gwithian and Portreath). The name refers, of course, to pollution such as ochre coming from the mines. All the Red Rivers are colourless these days and only the Carnon River earns the title now (early 1992), thanks to the flooding of Wheal Jane. Close to the road where it crosses the Red River are the impressive buildings of Boskennal Mill.

4 At the T-junction turn left. The road keeps close to the stream and eventually crosses it at a ford, but for the walk to Cripplesease you need to go through the metal farm gate on the right just before reaching the ford. *(To reduce the walk to about 3 miles, however, continue over the bridge by the ford and turn left at the road above, picking up the directions at point 13.)* The path runs uphill: after you have crossed a barbed-wire fence by means of a wooden "stile", walk up the quite steep, narrow path cut through tall gorse - a path which could quickly become impenetrable if neglected - in which case you would need to return to point 4 and turn left there, following the bridleways as indicated on my sketch-map and rejoining the directions at point 5. The path through the gorse ends at another wooden stile in another barbed-wire fence; then continue ahead beside the hedge on your right. At the top you get more fine views; ahead is the stony outcrop of Trencrom. After negotiating a gate, cut off the corner of the next field: head towards the church spire (St Hilary) on the skyline. Cross the "stile" (really just a bit of wooden fencing on top of a hedge), then walk across a long, narrow field to a low stile and a sunken path - actually a bridleway, as the deep mud along most of its length vividly testifies.

5 Turn left on that. In view of the straggly brambles and the aforementioned mud, we were quite glad when we eventually reached the road. Turn left there.

6 At the cross roads turn right *(or, to omit Cripplesease and the Engine Inn, reducing the walk by about a couple of miles, turn left, then right at the T-junction and along the valley road into Nancledra, picking up the directions at point 10).* Now comes quite a long but gentle walk up Brunnion Carn, for which you are rewarded by the ever-more-splendid view and the fine old cross on the left at the top. "At one time," says Craig Weatherhill in *Bellerion,* "it stood dramatically in the centre of a small pool of water" - but we were glad to sacrifice the drama in return for a chance to sit for a while on the granite base. The view is at its best when you reach the ruined engine house, as mentioned at the end of my introductory note. On the slope of Trink Hill, the less rocky of the two hills close by, is the Twelve o' Clock Rock, so called because according to legend "although it was quite impossible to move this stone during daylight, or indeed by human power at any other time, it would rock like a cradle exactly at midnight. Many a child has been cured of rickets by being placed naked at this hour on the twelve-o'-clock stone" (Robert Hunt: *Popular Romances of the West of England,* 1881). According to Tony Deane and Tony Shaw, however, it "takes its name from the sun striking on its side at midday, forming a rough sundial; but when the stone "hears" a cock crowing it turns itself around" (*The Folklore of Cornwall,* 1975). On the left of the road are restored buildings of a tin mine, one of which was originally the miners' dry (changing-room); the more imposing house was probably the mine's count house (offices). A path on the right leads to the engine house, beside which is a good example of a shaft complete with masonry lining. These are all relics of Wheal Margaret, part of a group of mines that became known as Wheal Sisters (*). Continue northwards along the minor road.

WHEAL SISTERS, with special reference to WHEAL MARGARET

Five old tin mines combined in 1875 as Wheal Sisters, a title which was chosen because three of them had girls' names, Margaret, Kitty and Mary; the other two were Old Tincroft and Trencrom Mine. Wheal Margaret was in production by 1782 and made very considerable profits in the following decades, but after 1862 it worked at a loss. Cyril Noall in *The St Ives Mining District,* Vol. 1, describes an accident at Wh. Margaret in 1851 when water in a shaft abandoned 50 years before broke in and cascaded through the newer workings. "It sent a blast of air before it which blew out most of the miners' candles, adding to the horror of their situation as they struggled to find their way out of the mine in total darkness." There were some amazing escapes, but also several horrific deaths. Noall tells of the severe flooding problems caused by the very wet winter of 1874-5: the workings of Wheal Mary were threatened by the inability of the pumps at Whs. Kitty and Margaret to cope with the water. After some months of quarrelling the problem was solved by the decision to amalgamate. Unfortunately the hopes of increased prosperity were dented by a serious fall in tin prices in the following years; although parts of the sett, particularly Wh. Mary, continued to be very productive the enterprise was closed down in 1890, and attempts to re-open the mines in 1906-8 came to nothing. The photograph on page 83 of Noall's book gives some idea of how this landscape has been transformed since the days, little more than a hundred years ago, when it was "dominated by the smoking stacks, roaring stamps and busy tinyards," and when about a thousand people depended directly or indirectly for their living on Wheal Sisters. Even the great burrows (waste tips) have now mostly gone, much of the material having been used in the building of the rerouted A30, and only two of the many engine houses have survived in recognisable form. (Kenneth Brown has listed as many as 24, one of which may have belonged to another mine.) The one you see on this walk contained a pumping engine - a small one by Cornish standards: 26in. with an 8ft. stroke. Wh. Margaret had another shaft and engine house on the other side of the road, and a tramway ran from that, crossed the road and followed roughly the course of the existing path, continuing eastwards to further shafts and the mine's dressing floors. For a little more about Wheal Sisters, see Walk 10, the route of which gives a good view of the other surviving engine house.

7 Turn left at the T-junction, then right at the main road (B3311). The name of the guest house opposite, "The Wink", may indicate that long before it started serving cream teas it was a "kiddleywink" or beer shop. (Kiddley-winks were not licensed to sell spirits, but if you gave a wink they could be had from the "kiddle" or kettle - so runs a popular but perhaps apocryphal explanation of the word.) The name of the hamlet, Cripplesease, apparently refers to the welcome sight of an inn after a long haul uphill. The Engine Inn has an apt name, unless perhaps it ought now to be "The Engine House Inn", since the 50-inch beam engine which used to occupy the building at Frank's Shaft, Giew Mine (*), is long gone. A short walk along the road would enable you to visit it. Though sadly neglected now and in use as a giant litter-bin - an inevitable consequence, I suppose, of being beside a layby on a main road - it is impressive and unusually complete: even the decorative iron frames have survived in some of the windows. Beside the main building, which bears the date 1871, are a wall of the boilerhouse, the concrete foundations of an electric power station and winder, and the remains of the earlier beam whim. A.C.Todd and Peter Laws considered Giew to be "perhaps the first mine that should be visited by the student who wishes to understand the cultural landscape of tin mining"; for their description of this site as it was in 1972, see *The Industrial Archaeology of Cornwall*. The folk at the Inn were busy preparing it for The Season when we visited it in February, so perhaps it's hardly surprising that it fell short of David Guthrie's glowing tribute in *Cornish Pubs.* Anyway, the "Engine Oil" - one of its cheapest brews - and the toasted sandwiches were good.

8 Cross the small stile just beside the pub (on the left side of the parking space by the door). You should be able to make out the line of the path running down the length of the field, heading just to the right of the square brick chimney in the valley. This is a relic of the large mill built at Giew Mine when it became part of St Ives Consols early this century. There are three impressive granite stiles. After crossing the third, turn left, heading directly towards the stack now: ignore the left fork a few yards later. The path, rather narrow and somewhat overgrown in places, passes right by the stack, and after a couple of gates brings you to a minor road.

GIEW MINE

This very old and productive tin mine has been worked under many different names since at least the mid-18th century. Its last period of activity began in 1908, when it formed part of St Ives Consolidated Mines. "Giew," write Todd and Laws, "was the very last of the tin mines to cease working in 1923, bringing this ancient industry to a complete stop for the first time in its history." Moves to reopen it were made in about 1928, but a fall in tin prices killed the scheme. J.H. Trounson in *The Cornish Mineral Industry* gives many details about the history of this mine, and argues that "very considerable opportunities yet exist in Giew for making further important discoveries." The name, by the way, is said with a hard G, and may derive from the Cornish *kew* or *gew,* a hollow or enclosure. It is, says T.F.G.Dexter, a frequent field-name, often given to the best field on a farm or the one nearest the house, the first one to be enclosed.

NANCLEDRA

"Cledry", as its name is said locally, although now relying mostly on agriculture is surrounded by old mines and quarries (granite and china clay), and its population and prosperity have tended to rise and fall with theirs over the past two or three centuries. The mining ceased in 1923 when Giew finally closed - the last mine in the St Ives area to do so. The piece about Nancledra in *The Cornwall Village Book* (W.I., 1991) tells how the local (Towednack) brass band, formed in the 18th century, had a struggle to survive "as young miners left to work in Australia and elsewhere." A few ruined buildings and many old shafts remain, but the unusually well-preserved set of Cornish stamps (known as the Locke stamps) in the Red River valley south-east of the village was dismantled in the early 1980s and re-erected by Clive Carter at the Geevor Mining Museum. Eight stamps powered by an 18-foot waterwheel, they "were working as late as 1945-50" according to A. C. Todd and Peter Laws, who include a photograph of them in their *Industrial Archaeology of Cornwall* (1972). Nancledra was for many years the home of Robert Morton Nance, a leading authority on the Cornish language and a Grand Bard of the Cornish Gorsedd.

9 Turn left on that, at the T-junction left again, past the local junior school, then first right at a farm with cottages: Amalebra, probably meaning "hill's edge". Ignore the next right turning (if you can resist the tempting names on the sign: Georgia, Embla, Amalveor! - you have a chance of visiting some of them on Walk 9), and walk on down beside the stream - the Red River again - into Nancledra (*).

10 Turn left past the garage and the old mill beside it, which was being restored early in 1992: a sluice gate was still in place beside the road, and the remains of the waterwheel could still be seen in the wheelpit at the back. A few yards later, cross the road and go up past the post office and toilets. Take the narrow path up on the left, indicated by a yellow arrow on a wooden post. After a stone stile, go round the left-hand edge of the field to a second stile, where another yellow arrow has been placed. Now the path continues uphill in a fairly straight line, and is clearly waymarked with more yellow arrows.

11 At the top of the hill turn sharp right on a well-trodden path running through a scrubby area. The OS map indicates "Shafts" on the right, and indeed we had been told in Nancledra that there were lots of "old men's" mine workings up here. Little, however, can be seen from the paths, and we didn't venture to try to push our way into the gorse and brambles; if you do decide to explore, please bear in mind that you may be trespassing, and that such places can be very dangerous. Soon you get another fine view ahead, including the Mount and Ludgvan church tower. The path opens out and becomes grassy. From somewhere near this point the official right of way runs between hedges a little to the left, but when we were here this was thoroughly overgrown and impenetrable. Unless it is cleared by now you will probably have to do as we did: climb over the low stone wall ahead which looked as if it had been quite recently erected, then keep beside the hedge on the left, cross the not-very-obvious stile in it (beside a ruined stone building), walk down through the gap, then go left to a rickety old metal gate which is close to a Public Footpath sign pointing to the overgrown path. From here according to the maps the path should continue downhill, but it appears to have been officially diverted, so walk beside the hedge on your left and through another gate where there is another Public Footpath sign.

12 Turn right on the road, and at the crossroads go straight on. A lot of building or rebuilding was taking place down by the stream when we were there. This is the Red River once more, and the Cornish stamps referred to in the note on Nancledra were here or close by. Turn left at the T-junction, past what appears to be a former watermill on the left (a leat seems to enter the stream a little lower down). This pretty valley road continues to run quite close to the Red River for about half a mile. At Ashtown Farm donkey rides are on offer at 2 p.m. every Saturday - even in February, as we witnessed; but whether the donkeys are capable of assisting weary walkers I'm not sure. Ignore the left turnings, the second of which goes down to the ford mentioned earlier. Down on the left is Boskennal Mill.

13 When you reach the farm of the same name, turn right at the main entrance and follow the wide farm track that passes among the buildings. There is a footpath sign just before an extremely muddy patch around metal gates; we found we could avoid the worst of the gunge by climbing the gate on the left side. At the wider area where tyres are dumped, go down the steepish path on the right. In the little copse below, cross the new-looking wooden stile on the right, then go left, where a wooden walkway enables you to cross a stream and boggy area. After a fairly steep climb, including a small wall to be scaled, the path continues uphill beside the hedge on the right. Go through the farm gate ahead - another rickety one, draped with barbed wire - and still walk beside the hedge till you reach the next gate. Don't go through that but turn left, keeping the hedge on your right. As you come to the gap in the hedge ahead it's best to go through or over the gate on your right, because a stile further on is now virtually unusable. Keep beside the hedge for a little longer, but the path cuts off the bottom corner of the field and leads to a wooden gate and a track which soon brings you to a road.

14 Turn left on that, past Menwidden ("whitestones") Farm, and turn right at the entrance marked "Wellway" and "Stile Cottage". The latter is aptly named, because there are three low stiles in quick succession beside it. At the third turn left and walk towards the church with the hedge on your left. After a footbridge between two more stiles the path runs just above a shallow little valley, then goes uphill for a few yards. From here on it's difficult to give accurate directions because of the complicated layout of small fields, many of them ploughed and planted with no attempt made to reinstate the path. The best rule is to keep heading straight for the church tower, and if you manage to follow the correct line of the path you will cross four stiles along the way. If, however, you find yourself on one of the several paths that wander down into the valley on your left, don't panic, because that simply means you will return to the church on the same path by which you set out.

WALK 3
PRUSSIA COVE, TREBARVAH, PERRANUTHNOE AND THE COAST

A little over four miles

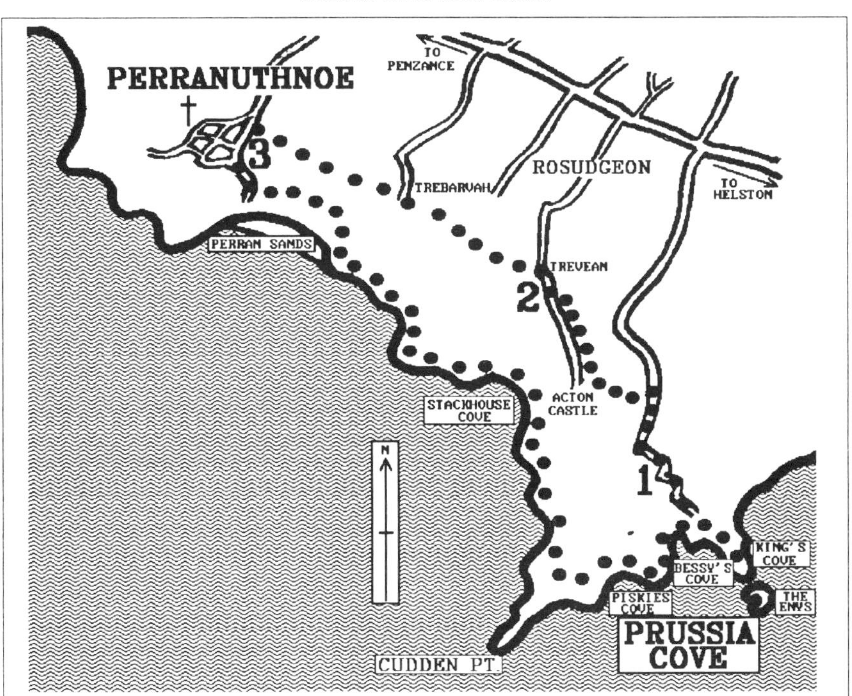

This is an easy little walk with a pleasant pub (and a good bathing beach if the weather's right for that) at the half-way point. The first half is through gently rolling countryside, farmland where spring flowers and early vegetable crops are grown, dotted here and there with the burrows of long-disused mines. For much of this part of the walk you have a fine view ahead of St Michael's Mount. The return along the coast begins with low cliffs, but gradually becomes more dramatic as you approach Cudden Point, and culminates with the group of rocky inlets collectively known as Prussia Cove. "Romantic" is the adjective that occurs most often in the older guidebooks, especially when describing Bessy's Cove; be that as it may, the place is certainly full of historical interest. As well as the pub mentioned above, Perranuthnoe has a shop and public toilets.

There is a convenient car park at Porthenalls, Prussia Cove (*). The Cove is signposted from the A394 Penzance-Helston road at Rosudgeon. Perranuthnoe has a car park near the beach, and you could equally well start and end the walk there, provided that you're happy to take a picnic with you or delay refreshments till the end of the walk. In that case, start reading the directions at point 3.

PRUSSIA COVE

Its old name was Porth Leah, perhaps meaning "cove of the flat rocks". It is really two coves, known as King's and Bessy's or Bessie's, separated by a small island called the Enez or Enys, a name which simply means "island". Bessy Burrow or Bussow is said to have been the owner of a beer house or kiddleywink on the cliffs above that cove, and it seems probable that another such establishment gave rise to the name "Prussia Cove". During and immediately after the Seven Years' War (1756-63), Frederick the Great, as Leslie Douch says, "was the darling of Protestant Europe," and "his representation appeared on many an inn-sign" *(Old Cornish Inns).* "The King of Prussia" still survives as a pub name in Fowey, but instead of the picture of Frederick which was originally used, the sign there now depicts, as Mr Douch puts it, "that renegade smuggler Carter of Bessy's Cove." John Carter (1738-1803) was among the most celebrated and successful smugglers in Cornwall; his brother Harry (1749-1829) was scarcely less so, and he is of special interest to us now because he wrote a remarkable autobiography which gives a vivid picture of his life and times. These secluded little coves in an area which was then very sparsely populated and inaccessible were well suited to the trade, and John Carter - invested in the popular imagination with the superhuman powers of a legendary hero - is said to have cut out little harbours and the "rutways" down to and across the rocks, adapted the caves as stores and created passages from them to his house on the clifftop. Some versions of the story claim that as a boy John resembled Frederick the Great in appearance and always took the part of Frederick in games, so was nicknamed "The King of Prussia"; others tell that to fool the authorities he acted as landlord of a pub of that name. Perhaps the substantial house he built himself, roughly where Porthenalls now stands, doubled as the pub. He called it the King's House, and the cove below presumably took its name from it. He is said to have mounted guns on the nearest headlands, and on one occasion to have opened fire on a revenue cutter, the *Fairy* .... "which thereupon sent its boats against the battery, and destroyed it", says an early version (Murray's Handbook, 1859); "which fled", says a recent one (J.H.N.Mason, *West Country Walks and Legends,* 1980). That is typical of the way the tales of John Carter have developed in the retelling, many of them portraying him as a man of honour and a latter-day Robin Hood robbing the rich to help the poor people of Germoe .... The best summary I have come across of the activities of "the Carter family firm" is that included in *Smuggling in Devon and Cornwall* by Mary Waugh (Countryside Books, 1991).

ACTON CASTLE

I have often considered trying to establish a claim to this mansion, but my branch of the Actons comes from Sussex, and Acton Castle derives its name from the Actons of Acton Scott in Shropshire, where the Elizabethan manor house still survives. The name "Stackhouse" (shown on the maps as the name of the cliff and cove below Acton Castle) provides a link with Treslothan, near Camborne. If you have done Walk 9 in *A View from Carn Brea* you will know the delightful little Victorian church of Treslothan, which was built by Edward W. Wynn-Pendarves. His surname before he inherited the Pendarves estates had been Stackhouse. Edward's father, John Stackhouse, of Trehane in the parish of St Erme, had become, through marriage, the owner of Acton Scott. (I am grateful to the former Vicar of Treslothan, Father Francis Sutcliffe, for providing much of the foregoing information.) Most guide books state that John Stackhouse himself built the mansion above Cudden Point in about 1775 and gave it his wife's maiden name, but it is possible, as Fr. Sutcliffe suggests, that he acquired it through his marriage and rebuilt it on the grand scale. Stackhouse was an eminent botanist, and is supposed to have valued Acton Castle as a convenient base to carry out his studies of seaweed. The house plays a part in the history of local smuggling, because in 1788 Harry Carter took refuge there for three months when he had a price of £300 on his head - and this was, presumably, with the connivance of John Stackhouse. (See the note on Prussia Cove.) During part of the 19th century Acton Castle belonged to Richard Lanyon, of the Kennall Gunpowder Works at Ponsanooth: see *A Second View from Carn Marth,* Walk 9. In recent years it has been a hotel; it is now divided into apartments and belongs to a construction company.

1 From the car park walk back along the road. Ignore the first signed footpath on the left (to Cudden Point), but take the next one, which starts at a low stile. Keep by the hedge on your left. The large building ahead is Acton Castle (*). Where the hedge curves left, go right, to another stile consisting of slate slabs above a cattle-grid. Now walk beside the hedge to the left again, and at the corner continue along the field edge, with the hedge separating you from the entrance drive to the "Castle". You cross two more stiles, still keeping the hedge on your left, and then finally cross the hedge at a stile with a footpath sign.

2 Turn right on the road, and very soon you are passing among the buildings of Trevean Farm. Ignore the footpath sign to the right: turn left past a ruined house, and when you come to more footpath signs turn right, through a gateway into a long field. A short distance to the right are the workings of Trevean Mine, which seems to have been too small an enterprise to have been noticed even by Collins or Dines, but which according to Hamilton Jenkin "enjoyed a short-lived celebrity" in 1847 when what seemed to be a rich vein of silver was discovered. No record of any sales of silver exists, however. Keep by the left-hand hedge; cross the stile at the end of the field, and now for a change the hedge is on your right, and the glorious view of Mount's Bay and the Mount itself is unobstructed.

WHEAL TREBARVAH

Several mines around Perranuthnoe were producing mainly copper in the last quarter of the 18th century; the most important was Wheal Neptune, near the buildings of Ednovean Farm, north-east of the village. A sett on land belonging to Trebarvah Farm was granted in 1785, under the name of Wheal Jenny. There are records showing that the mine was worked during the 1840s, its name by then changed to Wheal Jane; and from 1848 till 1861 it was operated by another company as Wheal Trebarvah. (Trying to trace the history of Cornish mines is often bedevilled by the frequent changes of name: apparently this mine was also called Wheal Castle at some point.) During this period it is recorded as having sold about 3,400 tons of copper ore plus some tin. In one last spell of activity during the 1870s it produced mainly iron ore.

Perranuthnoe Church can also be seen now. Ignore a stile on the right; continue ahead over another one and through a farmyard (Trebarvah, "middle farm"). After the metal gate, walk almost straight on, heading towards the Mount and the church. Cross a wooden stile on the left of a stone farm building, and then another wooden stile - and still you should be heading for the Mount and the church. A little further along, notice the old mine burrows (waste tips) on both sides, and down among a few bungalows on the left is a truncated chimney-stack. These are relics of Wheal Trebarvah (*). The path continues clear ahead, with the hedge on your right most of the way. As you approach the village of Perranuthnoe (*), follow the line of telegraph wires. Soon you are among the houses, and in no time you are treated to the sight of Ye Olde Victoria Inn. The granite village is pretty and immaculately kept, well worth exploring, as is the church.

3 To continue the walk, take the seaward road down through the village, passing the main car park and public toilets. Turn left at the acorn sign just past them, and when you come to Blue Burrow Cottage keep right. (The acorn sign there looks as if it may not have much more life in it.) Another sign point you right, and then a left turn brings you to the edge of the low cliffs, marked on the maps as Trebarvah Cliff. The tamarisks here must be a lovely sight in full flower. From here on, few if any directions are needed. You have several stiles to cross - one or two of them rather high and awkward. The first cove, Trevean, has a track down to the rocky beach on the far side, probably originally intended to enable horse-drawn carts to bring up sand to help neutralise the acid soils, and seaweed as a fertiliser. In this area, so famous for smuggling, another explanation also comes to mind.... Judging by the maps, there are several handy caves hereabouts, too; Favel's Hole and Long Zawn, for example, both just beyond Trevean Cove. The next cove, below Acton Castle, is called Stackhouse, which may suggest mining, but in fact refers to the family who owned the Castle in its early days. As you walk on, when you reach the National Trust sign, Cudden Point, look back to see an impressive cave or chasm, which I take to be Long Zawn. There are more caves on the west side of Cudden Point: Arch Zawn and Zawn Susan. A small path down to the right looks as if it might lead to one or both; you might care to explore the headland. A legend tells that

PERRANUTHNOE

Like Perranarworthal, the site of the great rival to Harvey's Hayle Foundry, Perranuthnoe has a name which links St Piran with the principal manor of the area: Arworthal there, Uthno or Udno here. It appears in the Domesday Book as Odenol. Among its earliest owners were the Whalesboroughs; in 1460 it passed through marriage to the Trevelyans: see the note on Goldsithney, Walk 4. The link with St Piran is a matter of conjecture. He is said to have arrived on the north Cornish coast from Ireland at the end of the 5th century, sailing across on a millstone. The church guide leaflet comments: "The legend has probably grown out of the small circular altar stone which Celtic monks carried about with them." Place names and the dedications of churches and holy wells suggest that he landed near Perranporth, passing through both the villages named Perranwell and finally Perranuthnoe on his way to Brittany. The tiny church he founded at Perranzabuloe was smothered by wind-blown sand; he may have built a similar one here, and if so it could well have been drowned, since there is evidence that the sea has advanced about a mile since his day. (An old Cornish name for St Michael's Mount means "grey rock in the wood": at exceptionally low tides the remains of a forest covering much of Mount's Bay are sometimes revealed.) A Norman church was built on the present site towards the end of the 12th century, and there are a few remnants of that: the font and the arches over two doors and the south transept. In the 15th century the north aisle was added, replacing a north transept, and the tower was heightened so that it would serve as a navigational aid. An interesting small detail is the much-worn carving of St James inside the church above the south door: see again the note about Goldsithney. Although the church leaflet does not mention a Victorian restoration, it was in fact very thoroughly given the J. P. St Aubyn treatment in 1883; Donald Rawe calls it "cruel" and Betjeman "brutal". The list of rectors, in the north aisle, has a point in common with the list of vicars at Gulval: a hint of the toll taken by the Black Death in 1348-9; and although Richard Astley's 52 years at Perranuthnoe can't really compare with William Wingfield's 73 at Gulval, it is interesting that they were such close contemporaries.

when the weather is right you can see a silver table below the surface. One of the Lords of Pengersick (at Praa) was feasting aboard his boat off Cudden when it suddenly sank, drowning all on board; if the day is still enough you should be able to hear them feasting still. Cudden Point certainly has witnessed many a shipwreck, the best known of which was that of the battleship *Warspite* when in April 1947 she was being towed to the breakers' yard. The skeleton crew on board was rescued by the Penlee lifeboat. The main path climbs and soon brings you to a good viewpoint at Little Cudden. Piskies Cove is in the foreground; in the middle distance are Praa Sands, with Rinsey and Trewavas Heads beyond; and in clear weather you should be able to run your eye along most of the coastline to Predannack Head and Kynance Cliff. Notice the Hottentot figs growing on the cliffs above the rocks and beach at Piskies Cove. This fleshy-leaved succulent, closely related to the Livingstone daisy (mesembryanthemum) so commonly seen in gardens, is a native of South Africa which seems to have been introduced to Cornwall towards the end of last century. It has established itself particularly well on the cliffs at Lizard Point. The pink and yellow flowers make a beautiful show from about May to July, but botanists look on the plant as a serious pest because it tends to smother native species, and also

Bessy's Cove

creates masses of dead material which becomes a fire hazard in dry summers. Soon you have a choice of paths; the coastal footpath is the lower one. Bessy's Cove, just beyond, is, I think, one of the most attractive and interesting places on this walk. It is overlooked by a little group of fishermen's sheds which look like a rare survival from mid-19th-century photographs, even if the "galvanise" roofs of some of them, held down with chains, speak of comparatively modern times. Murray's Handbook of 1859 includes the following: "A well-like chasm forms a shaft to the largest cave. Through this they (the fishermen) draw up their fishing gear from the shore, and by its means in the winter procure a number of starlings and other birds which have sheltered here to hybernate. When the mouth of the cavern has been closed by seaweed they stretch a net over the aperture above, and thus entrap the unwary visitors, and as many as 500 have been captured at once." Across the rocks below is perhaps the best example in Cornwall of a "rutway" (*). At low tide you could walk across the beach and rocks - well supplied with pools - to the far side of the cove; alternatively, use the paths around the clifftop. The inland track or lane soon brings you back to the car park; but before returning to your car, if you go through the impressive wooden gates you can walk through the buildings of Porthenalls (*) to King's Cove and Kenneggy Sands. To the right of a line of coastguards' cottages can be seen remains of a mine called Wheal Speedwell (*).

RUTWAYS

An interesting article by John Owen in the 1991 Journal of the Trevithick Society describes a number of sites in north-east Yorkshire where parallel grooves have been cut in foreshore rocks which are under water at high tide. In almost every case these are at places where minerals such as alum and ironstone needed to be loaded on to boats, and coal, potash and ammonia had to be brought ashore for the works and mines. Every "rutway" Mr Owen investigated had a gauge of 4ft 4ins, measured from the centre of each groove, with a very few exceptions, all of which were within two inches of that; and on a nearby farm he managed to find a worm-eaten cart of the correct age, the wheels of which were exactly 4ft 4ins apart, centre to centre, at the point of contact with the ground. He points out that such rutways would enable carts to be guided safely over the rocks even after dark and when their wheels were under water. Whether or not the rutway at Bessy's Cove was, as many writers claim, created by John Carter as part of his family's smuggling business, I don't know, but it is certainly an impressive example, being about 60 yards long and up to 16ins deep - and the ruts are 4ft 4ins apart.

In the sketch of Bessy's Cove, the rutway can (I hope) be seen, running across the rocks, starting near the small beach on the left.

The notes about Porthenalls and Wheal Speedwell are on page 30.

PORTHENALLS

Through the generosity of its owners, Mr and Mrs Tunstall-Behrens, Porthenalls ("cove of the cliff") has for the past twenty years been the home of the International Musicians' Seminar. Twice a year, around Easter and early autumn, young instrumentalists from all over the world gather at Prussia Cove to play in the company of "maestri" such as Ralph Kirschbaum, Steven Isserlis, Andras Schiff and Sandor Vegh. The last of those was the founder of the Seminar. In the early days, choral singing was involved, and members of local groups were welcome to join in, bolstering the numbers for public performances. I remember singing "The Childhood of Christ" in St Hilary Church, and feeling distinctly under-rehearsed but privileged to be admitted to the company of "real musicians". Although the concerts and recitals nowadays are purely instrumental, we are no less privileged: few if any musical occasions in Cornwall are more exciting than these, in which established soloists and chamber players share as equals with artists whose names are in many cases destined to become as familiar as theirs.

WHEAL SPEEDWELL

"Speedwell" is a common sort of name for a Cornish mine: an optimistic response to the considerable risks involved in launching the enterprise. Compare Goodluck, Good Fortune, Hope and Prosper: according to D. B. Barton no fewer than fifteen mines in Cornwall were given one or other of the last two names. This mine justified the risks better than most of those, since it is recorded as having produced over 11,000 tons of copper ore between 1819 and 1854, and according to one source had made a profit of £60,000 by 1843. Later plans to reopen the mine (1863 and 1872), however, seem to have come to nothing. Some of the workings of Wheal Speedwell go beneath the sea at a depth of 30 fathoms (180 feet). In *Mines and Miners of Cornwall,* Part 4, Hamilton Jenkin quotes a contemporary account of this mine during the 1820s, when it was at its most prosperous. As Jenkin says, it pictures a "comfortable, easy-going way of life" - but then, it is seen from the point of view of the son of the mine owner: "We had very much business at the Account House, money paid to the men twice a month, Copper Ore sampling every month, Tin Sales often, Owners' Account every two months - a good Dinner and dividends after, making it a very pleasant time. There were always Dinners at Pay Days, Sampling Days, etc. ...."

WALK 4
ST HILARY, HALAMANNING, GOLDSITHNEY and TREGURTHA DOWNS

About 4.5 miles

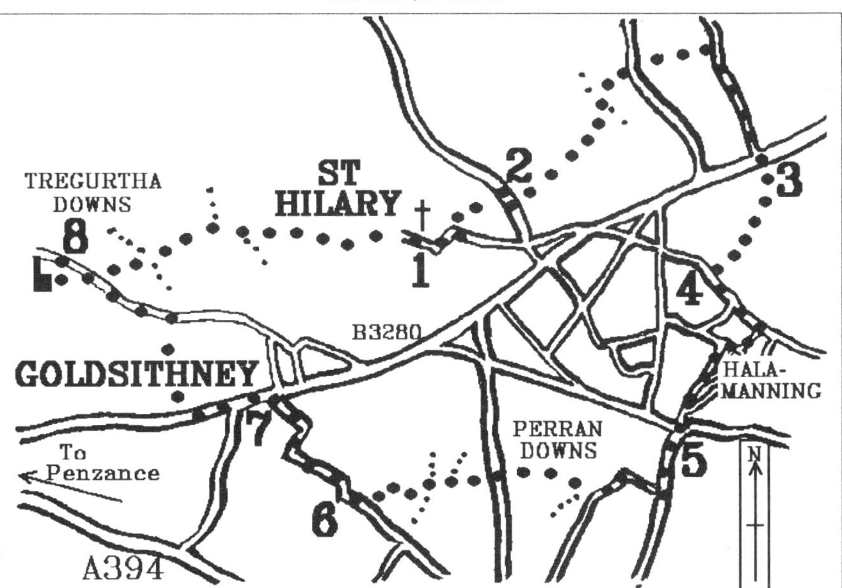

A visit to St Hilary will be immensely enriched by a reading of the autobiography of its most famous rector, Bernard Walke: "Twenty Years at St Hilary". Some information about the colourful and even dramatic events of those years is in my note about the church, and can also be found in the booklets by Horace Keast and B. E. Beach, both of which were on sale in the church when I was last there; but for its sensitive portrayal of the landscape and people of the area Father Walke's book is unrivalled. The walk is through pleasant countryside which still retains much evidence of 18th- and 19th-century mining. The attractive village of Goldsithney, which has two contrasting pubs as well as shops, is conveniently placed about half-way along the route if you start and end at St Hilary church. The going is generally easy, with no steep hills, but the path may be rather overgrown at Perran Downs and near the end of the walk, and muddy at Trevabyn Farm.

There is room for a few cars to park at St Hilary church (*). St Hilary Churchtown is signposted from the B3280 (Redruth-Penzance) road a short way north-east of Goldsithney. From Hayle it can be reached by minor roads via St Erth and Penberthy Cross.

1 Leaving the churchyard by the main gate, turn left. The avenue of trees on the right, planted during the very long incumbency of Rev. Thomas Pascoe (1758-1814) and severely damaged by a storm in 1929, was nicknamed

ST HILARY CHURCH

The spire is visible from the sea and used to be whitewashed to make it more useful as a landmark for sailors. Horace Keast, author of the church guide, suggests that the decision to build a spire was made by the Norman monks of St Michael's Mount, who appointed a French master-mason to build the church: he points out that most, if not all, old Cornish churches with spires show French influence. He argues that the choice of a 4th-century Bishop of Poitiers as patron saint also resulted from this French connection. Little remains of the 14th-century building except the tower and spire, because the rest was destroyed by fire in 1853, although some of the original stone was used in the rebuilding that followed. St Hilary became nationally famous during the incumbency of Bernard Walke (1913-36), whose strong leanings towards Roman Catholicism, as well as his pacifism during the "Great War", scandalised many, but who also earned respect for his dedication and integrity, and love for his human warmth and generosity. His wife Annie was an artist, and he embellished the church with paintings by her and some of the leading local artists who were their friends; Annie's picture of St Joan is there still. A tradition grew up of performances in the church of plays written by Father Walke and acted by the parishioners with singing and dancing by the children; the Christmas play, "Bethlehem", went out on "the wireless" each year and became for a while as much of a seasonal institution as the King's College Festival of Nine Lessons and Carols is now. The large house near the church which in the mining days had flourished as a pub called The Jolly Tinners was converted into a home for children from poverty-stricken London families, and much of the cost of running the home was met through an appeal made at the end of the first broadcast. Walke's time at St Hilary was eventually marred, however, by an outburst of violent Protestant hostility culminating in August 1932 when (in Keast's words) "a coachload of hired labourers" tore down and destroyed everything in the church that was seen as tainted by Popery. Some items, such as the St Joan and St Frances paintings, the statues of St Anne and St Joseph, and the 15th-century Flemish painting in the Chapel of the Sacred Heart, survived because they were removed before the attack took place. Valiant efforts were made to restore as much as possible afterwards, but Walke's health rapidly deteriorated and he retired in 1936. His last five-or-so years were spent at Mevagissey, and his friend Frank Baker has written about his life there in *The Call of Cornwall.* A long "Low Church" period followed, during which John Betjeman visited: he found it a "barren, sad place". St Hilary has, however, reverted to something of the character it had in Walke's period under its last two rectors. The last section of Keast's guide gives information about the details in the church, among the most interesting being the paintings on the choir-stall panels, done by artists of the Newlyn School, and those on the parclose screen in the Lady Chapel, by the ten-year-old Joan Manning-Sanders. Relics of the Roman occupation include a 4th-century "milestone" inside the church and a stone mysteriously inscribed "Noti Noti" in the graveyard, where there are also several old Celtic crosses.

"The Cathedral" by Bernard Walke, and each August at the Feast of the Assumption of the Blessed Virgin there was a procession along it from the church to an open-air altar in the garden behind the vicarage. (The old vicarage was, Mr C.J.Rogers believes, occupied for a time by an "Art Commune" including Denys Val Baker. It became a private hotel after a period as a Land Army hostel, and a new vicarage was built behind it.) Take the second signed footpath on the left, between houses called "Tranquille" and "Jasmine Cottage" (unless by now their owners have had new inspirations). *Before starting on the footpath, however, you might care to go on a few yards to look at the old buildings of St Hilary Churchtown, some of which at various times served as stables, a small school, wheelwright's and carpenter's shops and a general store. The imposing house just beyond the cottages was a pub called The Jolly Tinners.* The path bends right, behind the cottages, and after the stile it runs diagonally across the field to another stile just left of the house at the corner.

2 Turn right on the road, then take the track on the left, where there is another footpath sign. Just after the farm buildings at Trelease, the track curves left. At the field entrance turn right ("90°", according to my notes, though I don't remember measuring it), and walk with the hedge on your left. Cross the road and the stile opposite and continue beside the hedge on your left. The path reaches a minor road just left of a cottage; turn right there.

3 Cross the B3280 with care and continue ahead for a few yards along a track. Take the signed path on the right, starting at a low stile beside a gate.

Keep beside the hedge on your left at first, but then cross another low stile beside the garden of a bungalow and walk on with the hedge on your right. Look left to see Godolphin and Tregonning Hills. Just after a left curve in the hedge and path, cross the stile over the hedge. The path now runs through an area of bracken, gorse and heather typical of many old Cornish mine setts.

4 At the wider track go left, and take the track on the right just before the first cottage. This soon brings you to a minor road. Notice the former Count House (offices) of Halamanning Mine (*). A vivid description of the Halamanning area is given by Frank Baker in *The Call of Cornwall;* he had a strong impression that it was "haunted", or "the centre of a psychic complex". Turn right and take the third track on the left, beside a line of telegraph poles, with old mine dumps on the right and the greenhouse of a nursery further along. Soon you are on a pleasant, leafy track running among a few houses and cottages.

5 At the road (Colenso Cross) go straight ahead, then take the first right turning. Soon this road bends left and passes a few modern bungalows; just past them, take the right-hand track of the two that come in from the right (called Grove Lane, though it is not named at the start). The area you are now passing through, known as Perran Downs, "was," writes A. K. Hamilton Jenkin, "worked for centuries by little groups of miners operating on their own account, there being a time, according to tradition, when a hundred windlasses might have been seen here at once, turning above as many shafts."

HALAMANNING MINE

Halamanning and Retallack, a little to the east, were already important copper mines by the 1780s. A 40-inch Boulton & Watt engine was erected at Halamanning in 1778 (only a year after the first B & W engine in Cornwall, at Chacewater Mine) and replaced by a 60-inch one when the first was moved to Retallack in 1786. A poor impression of the way Halamanning was run is given by a letter Boulton wrote to Watt in 1784 saying that the engines there "abound with dirt, sin and misery" although the mine itself was still good. Another point of special interest to historians of Cornish engines is that Edward ("Ned") Bull erected at Halamanning one of the inverted engines which were to be the subject of a breach-of-patent action brought against him by Boulton and Watt: see *The Landfall Book of the Poldice Valley,* page 65. A 1787 report on the mine refers to numerous shafts and levels, and a map dated 1791 indicates 36 shafts along the course of the main adit, which was a mile-and-a-half long. Despite selling ores to the value of £26,671 between 1793 and 1796, however, the mine seems to have closed before the turn of the century. When it was re-opened (1831-6) it was not very successful, although the discovery of some tin compensated for the declining output of copper. 13,400 tons of copper ore were sold by Halamanning and Croft Gothal in 1851-8, but when the mine closed in 1860 it had made a loss of £100,000. That seems to have been the end of mining here apart from some small-scale operations in 1912. (The name, Halamanning, apparently means "butter moor" - one of those explanations which just raise new questions!)

During the 19th century various small companies mined hereabouts, among them East and West Trevelyan Mines, Nanturras Mine and West Wheal Charles. At the road, continue on the track opposite, which later becomes a narrow path. At the T-junction turn left, and where the path divides take the right fork. The path passes to the right of a house, and then reverts to a wider track before reaching the road.

6 Turn right on that. On the left now you get a glimpse of St Michael's Mount, and ahead is the restored engine house of Tregurtha Downs mine. Keep to the "main" road as it curves right and left into Goldsithney (*). As mentioned at the start, the two pubs here are very different: the Crown Inn on the sunny (if you're lucky) side of the street attracts customers from miles around and has an extensive menu, whereas the Trevelyan Arms is a typical "local" with a homely atmosphere and good plain food. You don't have to forego sitting in the sun there, because it has a pleasant garden at the back.

7 Turn left, down the main street of the village, passing the Trevelyan Arms on your left and Wesley Cottage on your right, and take the signed footpath

GOLDSITHNEY

Goldsithney was on the medieval pilgrim route to St Michael's Mount, and a lodging- and refreshment- house for pilgrims is said to have been where St James' House now is. Because of the great shrine of St James at Compostella in Galicia, his name became almost synonymous with pilgrimages, so it is not surprising that the Chapel erected at the centre of the village between 1400 and 1403 was dedicated to him. Charles Henderson, writing some time between 1910 and 1924, notes that it was apparently still standing in 1694, but says he could find no relic of it apart from "the little stone effigy of St James now set over the south door of the parish church" (Perranuthnoe). The name of the village itself also has a connection with St James. It was recorded in 1399 in the form "Pleyn-Goylsithny", meaning "St Sithney's fair-place": some time before 1284 the fair originally held at Sithney on St James's Day each year was moved here. Goldsithney Charter Fair takes place on 5th August (in practice nowadays, the first Saturday in August); St James's Day is 25th July, but the discrepancy merely reflects the change brought about by the adoption in Britain of the Gregorian Calendar (1752). The name of the Trevelyan Arms also recalls Goldsithney's past: as the W.I.'s *Cornwall Village Book* puts it, "History has it that the Trevelyan family were largely responsible for the foundation of the community." The Trevelyans acquired the Manor of Uthno by marriage in 1460; the legend that a Trevelyan was the sole survivor from the lost land of Lyonesse is alluded to on the family coat of arms, which forms the inn sign. Polsue in *Lake's Parochial History* called Goldsithney a "large and respectable village", but the anonymous author of the article in the W.I. book complains that it is now "a town without town facilities", since the growth of new housing estates has greatly increased its population, and yet the village school and many of the shops have closed. Mr C.J.Rogers tells me, however, that the old village hall, a "galvanise" structure affectionately known as "The Tin Tabernacle", has been replaced with a modern building which is used by many active local groups.

on the right. This takes you beside a housing estate and past the Cricket Club. After the kissing gate turn left and then keep to the main track till you come to a stile on the left. By this time you are close to the engine house of Tregurtha Downs mine (*), and the rather narrow and possibly overgrown path runs close beside it. When we were there last it was also possible to get back to the original track by walking beside the separate stack, but I don't think this is a right of way, so you may have to retrace your steps back to the stile. *(Those interested in Cornish mining may wish to walk to the chimney stack a short way along the track to the north. This belonged to the horizontal engine which drove the pneumatic stamps for Tregurtha Downs. Another stack further north belonged to Trevarthian Downs mine.)*

Tregurtha Downs

8 Turn right on the track - that is, back the way you came - and cross the wooden stile on the left, just past a metal farm gate. Cross the field to a group of farm gates, over a cattle-grid beside a post with yellow arrows, and then immediately over the wooden stile ahead. Now follow the direction shown by the yellow arrow on the stile: walk fairly near the hedge on the left, making for a small gap just left of a farm gate. Here another arrow points you through the narrow gap into the next field. Walk by the hedge on the left and keep left of the farm buildings at Trevabyn, where you are likely to have to negotiate mud and slurry. A small mine called Wheal Trevabyn, just south-east of the farm buildings, produced some copper between 1826 and 1832. The degree of its success can be gauged by the fact that its 21-inch engine had to be sold off in about 1828 to pay the miners' wages. After two more stiles you join a farm track for a while. Don't follow the red arrow (right) unless you want to return to Goldsithney: the yellow one (ahead) directs you towards St Hilary. After a stone cattle-grid the path runs beside the hedge on the left to a further stile/grid, where another arrow point you to the left - and if you see the church spire ahead now you're still (amazingly!) on the right track. A few nettles may impede your progress; even so, you should soon be passing the nicely-restored old houses near the church and reaching the church itself.

TREGURTHA DOWNS MINE

This mine plays a prominent part in the story of the Cornish beam engine. Under the name of Wheal Union (referring to the uniting of Tregurtha Downs with the nearby Owen Vean Mine as one company), it was the first Cornish mine to place an order with Boulton & Watt for an engine as large as 63-inch (July/September 1777); she started work a year later. (Like ships, beam engines are usually graced with the feminine gender.) In 1781 this engine was moved to a mine called Castle (or Kestal) Adit ("site not identified", state Dickinson and Jenkins in their *James Watt and the Steam Engine),* and by 1794 she was at Wheal Rose near Scorrier, east of Redruth. Better known, perhaps, is the engine employed at Tregurtha Downs during its last periods of working (about 1883-1902), described by Jack Trounson as a "beautiful 80in. diameter cylinder Cornish pumping engine" which "often had to run at exceptional speed in winter time" because the mine was an unusually wet one. I am quoting from *Mining in Cornwall,* Volume 2 (Moorland Publishing), which includes a fine photograph showing the engine house and stack, together with other mine buildings, as they were then. The engine was built in 1854 at Copperhouse Foundry, Hayle, for the nearby Alfred Consols; she later worked at Crenver & Wheal Abraham (Crowan) and was eventually bought by Tregurtha Downs in 1881, "1,200 spectators gathering to see the arrival of the bob, weighing 40 tons, pulled by forty-five horses." (Todd and Laws: *Industrial Archaeology of Cornwall)* A disastrous fire in 1889 gutted the engine house ("a column of fire one hundred feet high illuminated the hills of the entire district", writes Cyril Noall, who gives a graphic account of the almost comic attempts of the Marazion and Penzance fire brigades to cope with the emergency in *Cornish Mine Disasters),* but the engine was relatively unscathed and with a few minor repairs, together with a rapid re-build of the engine house, was back at work within a week. In 1903 she was bought (price: £375) by South Crofty Mine, between Redruth and Camborne, and worked there on Robinson's Shaft continuously day and night till 1955, thus qualifying as the last beam engine to work at a Cornish mine. Though her work is done now by electric pumps, the fine old "Robinson's" engine is still *in situ* at Crofty, under the care of the National Trust. The plan, mentioned by Trounson, to return the engine to Tregurtha Downs as the nucleus of a working mining museum has, clearly, been dropped, but the possibility of such a museum at Robinson's is still alive. The engine house at Tregurtha Downs resembles the even more imposing one at East Wheal Rose lead mine (Newlyn East - visited on a walk in *A View from St Agnes Beacon);* the London architect who designed it is said to have wanted it to look like a Cornish chapel. A photograph showing it before conversion is in Todd and Laws' book. Some details of the long history of Tregurtha Downs mine itself, which produced both tin and copper, are given by Hamilton Jenkin; he describes, for example, the laborious system operating in 1779, when the ore had to be taken by pack-horses two miles to the St Erth valley for stamping and dressing, returned to Tregurtha Downs for calcining (roasting, to drive off impurities such as arsenic) and then transported all the way to Calenick, near Truro, to be smelted.

WALK 5

ST ERTH AND THE HAYLE RIVER

About 7 miles, but several shorter versions can be done.

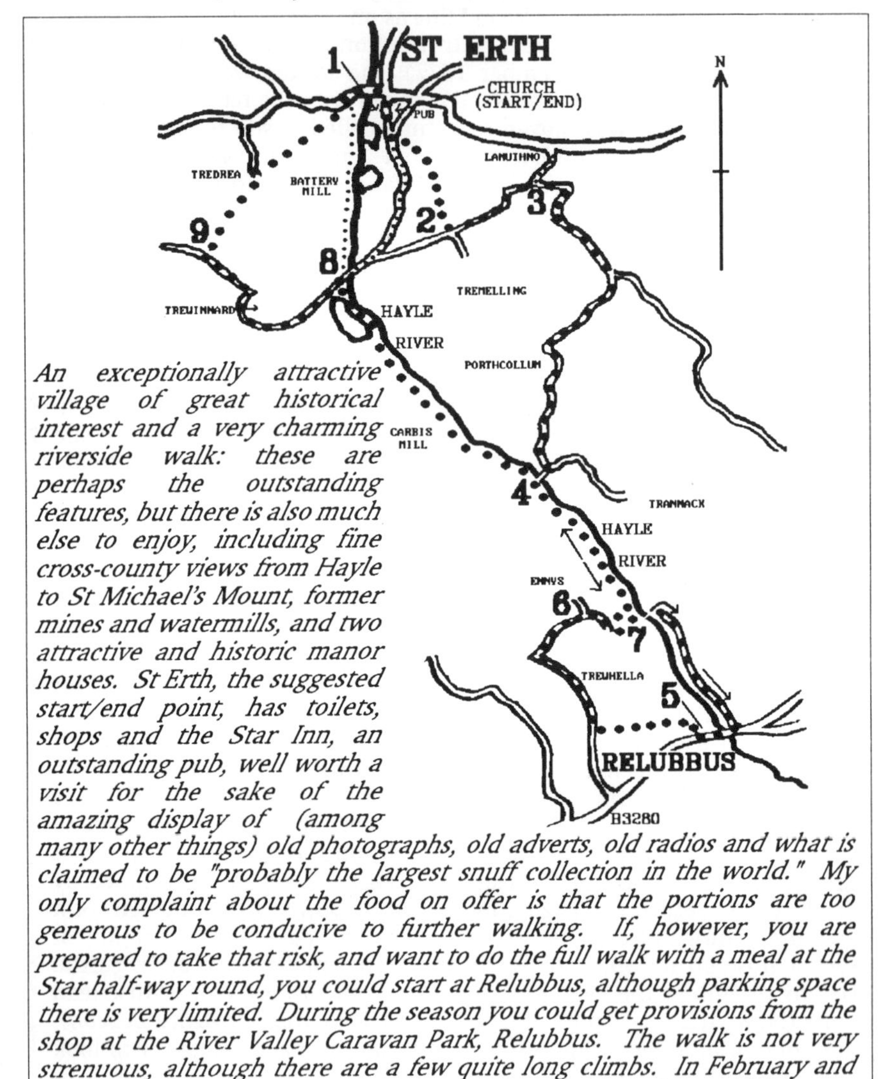

An exceptionally attractive village of great historical interest and a very charming riverside walk: these are perhaps the outstanding features, but there is also much else to enjoy, including fine cross-county views from Hayle to St Michael's Mount, former mines and watermills, and two attractive and historic manor houses. St Erth, the suggested start/end point, has toilets, shops and the Star Inn, an outstanding pub, well worth a visit for the sake of the amazing display of (among many other things) old photographs, old adverts, old radios and what is claimed to be "probably the largest snuff collection in the world." My only complaint about the food on offer is that the portions are too generous to be conducive to further walking. If, however, you are prepared to take that risk, and want to do the full walk with a meal at the Star half-way round, you could start at Relubbus, although parking space there is very limited. During the season you could get provisions from the shop at the River Valley Caravan Park, Relubbus. The walk is not very strenuous, although there are a few quite long climbs. In February and March there were a good many muddy patches, but nothing very bothersome.

St Erth is signposted from the A30 a short way west of Hayle. There is usually ample parking between the church and the river, but you may have to park elsewhere during times of services. Relubbus, if you decide to start there, is on the B3280 Redruth-Goldsithney road, about two miles from Goldsithney.

1 From the car park almost opposite St Erth (*) church, walk south along the Green Lane - that is, keep the church on your left. Notice, just beyond the churchyard, a concrete shed on the left inscribed "31.10.1943 Built by P.o.W." *For the shortest round walk - only about a mile - simply continue down the lane, cross the bridge and return beside the river, as described at the start of point 8; or at the bridge you could pick up the directions at point 8 line 6 and increase the walk to about two miles. A point of interest along the Green Lane is the fish farm, St Erth Fisheries, "where visitors can catch their own trout". A further possibility would be to walk in Tremelling Wood, which is a nature reserve in the care of the Cornwall Trust for Nature Conservation. For that, don't cross the bridge but turn left and walk upstream beside the river for about 50 yards, then climb the bank on your left. Various paths wander through the wood, which covers about six acres. Here and there the ground is marshy, and you may have to jump or paddle across a small stream. Long ago the river itself flowed through this area, and the uneven ground is a result of tin streaming. In addition to the usual spring flowers and autumn fungi, the woods contain some specimens of royal fern and a patch of Cornish moneywort. Further information about the nature reserve may be obtained from the wardens, Dr and Mrs A.P.Lewis, at Tremelling Cottage (0736- 753124).* For the longer routes, turn left - not up the road which cuts sharply back and leads to the pub, but a few yards further on, along a concreted track opposite the entrance to a site owned by the Marazion Angling Club. The track leads to a gate, beyond which is a group of tumbledown concrete-block buildings, surely due for demolition. One of them sports a low tower. These are the remains of the Prisoners of War camp where the builder of that shed was once incarcerated. Take the path on the right just before the gate. It starts at a granite "stile", perhaps more properly called a cattle grid, and the path is easy to follow. It runs beside hedges most of the way, and crosses four more similar grids before reaching a rather muddy lane. (It is called Tremellin Lane and leads to the farm of the same name, which means "Mill Farm". The mill was presumably at a lower level than the farm buildings.)

2 Turn left up the lane. After about a quarter of a mile you have a fine view to the left: even on the misty day when I did this walk, Lelant Saltings and Church were visible, and the Towans at the mouth of the Hayle River.

3 *At the road (Porthcollum Lane) you might care to make a short diversion to the left to see what the OS maps mark as an ancient "settlement" at Lanuthno (or Lanuthnoe). It is on the left as you approach the T-junction (St Erth Hill), and the roads themselves appear to run in what was once part of the circular ditch. There's little left to see now, apart from a level platform on a typical hilltop site with very long views, including Trencrom and a glimpse of St Michael's Mount. Flint flakes and an arrowhead have been found nearby at Lanuthno Farm. The name, Lanuthno, suggests an enclosed graveyard, possibly a monastic site; for a comment on this, see the note on St Erth.*

For the main walk route turn right along the minor road, from which the views are very good, with the Mount almost straight ahead. The name, Porthcollum or Porthcollumb, may mean "pool bare of shelter"; I'm not sure about the pool, but the windy, rainy March weather when I was here certainly

ST ERTH

Until Hayle Causey (Causeway) was built (1825) St Erth was the lowest bridging point on the River Hayle, and St Erth bridge carried the London-Penzance highway. John Leland described St Erth bridge in 1538: "a litle byneth the paroche church that stondith on the est side of the haven. This bridge was made a 200 yeres syns, and hath a 3 arches. Afore ther was a fery. Ther cam to this place ons, the haven beyng onbarrid, and syns chokid with tynne workes, good talle shippes." The present four-arched bridge dates mainly from the 17th century, according to Henderson, who mentions that maintaining it was always very costly because of its narrowness and the long causeway spanning marshy ground at each end. In 1816 Davies Gilbert of Tredrea had it widened. The fact that the river was easily navigable as far as St Erth "haven" until tin-streaming clogged it up would have made it a natural place for early seafarers to land and settle, including Irish or Welsh "saints" of about the 6th century, who may have been attracted as much by the mineral wealth of the valley as by the wealth of souls needing salvation. The old name for the settlement, Lanuthno or Lanuthnoe, has led to speculation that the earliest church was built by a missionary called Uthinock, or something similar. It has been suggested that the original "lan" (enclosed cemetery or chapel-site) was on St Erth Hill, perhaps occupying the site of the ancient round or hill fort just above Lanuthnoe Farm. In some ways this makes a better position for the church than the one which is presumed to have been chosen by "Erc, son of Deagh" (424-514), baptised in old age by St Patrick and created Bishop of Slane, because the present church is only about ten feet above sea level and has always been subject to flooding. This is probably why the bases of the pillars inside are hidden: the floor-level has had to be raised. Although most of the building dates from the 14th and 15th centuries, one relic of an earlier, Norman, structure was discovered under the floor when the church was restored in 1874: an ancient font, now in use again for its original purpose. Further investigation of what lies under the floor is proceeding as I write: see the article on the opposite page, reproduced from "The West Briton" of 12th December 1991. The church was heavily restored in 1747 as well as by the Victorians, but the later work was done by J.D.Sedding, and John Betjeman comments, "Compared with the brutal "restorations" J.P.St Aubyn was doing to old churches in the district at the time, this dark and holy little place must be one of the first really sensitive restorations in Britain." Notice the fine carved woodwork in the main nave roof; the memorial tablet to Davies Giddy (Gilbert) in the south aisle; and the beautiful Trewinnard Chapel, which dates from 1912. Outside, the grotesque animal-head carvings on the tower are worth a look, and the churchyard ("a pleasure to behold," said A.G.Langdon; "more like a municipal garden," said Betjeman) contains the head of one old cross, the shaft of another, and several interesting graves, for example of the Harvey and Trevithick families. (Richard Trevithick, the engineer, was married in this church but was buried in a pauper's grave at Dartford, Kent.) Lack of space in a book designed to be portable precludes comments on the village itself, which is rich in attractive and interesting features; but some of these are mentioned in the walk directions.

Dig starts for Celtic church

AN ARCHAEOLOGICAL dig for what could be the remains of a Celtic church has begun underneath the picturesque 14th century church at St. Erth.

Experts from the archaeological department of Exeter University, led by St. Erth parishioner Mr. Jim Navin, have started weekend explorations after the remains of an earlier church were discovered when chorister Rose Watson began to fall through a collapsing chancel floor.

"The most exciting find was that the pillars of the present church are standing on the walls of a previous church — it could be Norman it could be earlier," said the Vicar, the Rev. Tony Neal.

It was thought there had been three churches on the site — the present one, a Norman church and possibly a Celtic church.

But Mr. Neal said: "This whole area has been so mucked about in previous generations that they may well have ruined any trace of a Celtic church, but we are hoping against hope."

If the remains of a Celtic church are revealed, it is hoped to incorporate viewing panels in the chancel floor when it is replaced. No matter what is discovered, it seems certain parishioners will face a hefty bill to make good the floor area.

Mr. Neal said that they had already spent £110,000 on the church and would now have to start fund-raising again.

confirmed the rest. After Trenedros farm, ignore the left turning (Countess Bridge Lane). As the road starts descending towards the river, notice the "burrows" (waste heaps) created by mining in the shallow valley to the right, with Tremelling farm beyond. The mine here was called Wheal Squire; Dines gives details of its workings, but says there are no known records of the mine's production. Soon you pass the attractive buildings of the two Porthcollum farms. It is thought that there used to be an old chapel and graveyard here: an old building has been identified as likely to be the remains of it, and lead coffins were discovered nearby. This has prompted some people to interpret "Collumb" as a reference to the Celtic saint who has lent his name to two parishes near Newquay. According to the 1975 issue of the journal *Cornish Archaeology* there is a "tradition of a considerable settlement" at Porthcollum. I understand that a "dig" is currently under way here, but I saw no sign of it when walking by. After a patch of rather boggy woodland you reach the River Hayle (*).

4 Cross the footbridge. Now you have another opportunity to shorten the walk by turning right; in that case, pick up the directions in line 3 of section 7. For Relubbus turn left. The path runs by the canalised river, which when we were last there was quite fast-flowing, very clear, and full of long, bright green and red waterweeds streaming like mermaids' hair. Here and there tall rushes grow, but these had mostly just been "strimmed" at that time. Eventually you pass through a kissing gate, which marks the boundary of the River Valley Caravan Park. The big old house up on the right is called Ennys, from the Cornish word for an island; Oliver Padel explains that where this name (more commonly "Enys") is used inland it nearly always

THE RIVER HAYLE

This quiet and attractive stream, a haven now for walkers, horse-riders, canoeists, anglers and courting couples, was, not so very long ago, the setting and to a large extent the power-source for several mines, corn mills, a fulling mill and a copper-rolling mill; most of all, tin streaming. A photograph published in a supplement by one of the local papers in the week I am writing this brings home very forcibly the extent of the changes the river has seen. "St Erth valley alluvial working," reads the caption. "Steam shovel and tramway." The photograph is undated, but a similar one included by R.D.Penhallurick in *Tin in Antiquity* is dated about 1930. Dines, in *The Metalliferous Mining Region of South-West England*, explains that during the 1939-45 war "the deposits, consisting of sand and gravel with a peaty layer, were systematically bored from St Erth church to three-and-a-half miles upstream". This would explain why so much of the river now looks like a canal; and the ponds and marshy tracts just south of the church were created when "most of the area ..... was worked away by hydraulic sluicing and gravel pumps." The workings between St Erth and Carbis Mill yielded 55 tons of black tin, mainly in 1944; the section south of that to Relubbus and east from there was worked a little earlier and produced 31 tons. In all, over 250,000 cubic yards of material were removed during that period. (I wonder if the P.o.W.s were employed in this enterprise.) Long before the steam shovels and gravel pumps moved in, the part of the river included in this walk must have borne the scars of tin-streaming activities: George Henwood, for example, wrote in 1873 of streamers using a steam engine for drainage near St Erth bridge; and the excavations of 1927-30 revealed a stone axe about 12 or 14 feet down in the tin gravel, "eloquent testimony," concludes Mr Penhallurick, "of an early tin-streaming enterprise." The axe, now lost, is thought to have been between 3,000 and 4,000 years old.

refers to land beside a river. The number of ducks on and around the water increased as we approached the main buildings on the Caravan Park, supplied with "alternative energy" by both a windmill and a waterwheel. Cross the footbridge and continue along the road, turning right at the T-junction (B3280) into Relubbus (*). Many of its old cottages - probably once the homes of miners - have now been attractively restored, and the village pump is still there beside the 1875 Wesleyan Chapel, now converted into a house.

RELUBBUS

The first syllable of this name indicates that there was a ford here; the rest probably derives from a personal name. The ford would have been important, because the main pilgrim route to the Mount crosses the River Hayle here. There has been a bridge for at least seven centuries: a document of 1300 refers to the "Bridge of Gorlyn" (Gurlyn Farm is about half a mile away), and a stone bridge at "Relobis" is mentioned in 1613. The importance of the road and probably also of the alluvial tin in the river during the period of the Roman occupation is suggested by the fact that there was a small Roman camp at Bosence, a short way to the east.

The village well and pump at Relubbus

5 Turn right just beyond that, where there is a Public Footpath sign. The wide track bends left and passes through very pleasant, gently rolling countryside. If you look back from this point you can see at least two old stacks; these are relics of a small mine called Tregembo, which produced 112 tons of tin during the 1880s. A small pumping engine house was recently demolished, and not a trace remains. Cross the stile ahead and continue with the hedge on your right, cross two stone cattle-grids (with care, because they can be slippery), and at the minor road turn right. The spire on your left now is St Hilary church. The road passes Trewhella Farm, with its palm tree and thatched cottage, and then bends right. At this point, notice (ahead) the fenced mine-shafts. These are workings of a mine called Ennys Wheal Virgin (*). Go through the gate marked Ennys and along a tree-lined drive. Ahead now is Tregonning Hill, with Godolphin Hill on its left.

6 Turn right at the sign Ennys Cottage, where there is a yellow waymark arrow. A grassy track follows, and then another arrow directs you left over a wooden stile. You are now back on the property of the River Valley Caravan Park, and a notice asks for dogs to be kept on leads. As you walk down the surfaced road, notice the remains of mine burrows (waste heaps), more relics of Wheal Virgin, now landscaped and in use as caravan sites. Don't miss the right turning where there is a small footpath sign on a tree. Soon you pass the reception area and shop.

7 Turn left immediately before the footbridge and walk beside the river as before. (If you have started the walk at Relubbus, see section 4 for a few comments about this part of the walk.) Continue ahead when you get to the footbridge from Porthcollum. On the left soon are the remains of a pond, possibly the millpool for Carbis Mill (*), and an old leat (artificial

ENNYS WHEAL VIRGIN AND OTHER LOCAL MINES

Many of the mines beside the River Hayle are very old, but records of their activities and outputs are mostly scanty. They produced mainly copper, plus some tin and small amounts of lead and iron. Ennys Wheal Virgin exploited the lodes beneath the site of the present caravan park. Its workings were linked to those of Gurlyn Mine on the east side of the river; and very close, if not actually connected, to Wheal Virgin on the north side was Penberthy Crofts Mine. The last of these, which first recorded an output of copper in 1798, included older mines such as Wheal Fancy, Wheal Cock, Wheal Mundic, Treveneague Bal and Kestal Bal. Kestal Bal later became Wheal Friendship and included yet another mine called Wheal Guskus or Anna and Guskus. Treveneague and Kestal Farms are quite distant from Penberthy; Hamilton Jenkin gives some details about the various adits used to drain this large area, and the waterwheels and "fire engines" that assisted the process in the latter part of the 18th century: "No less than 63 shafts," he writes, "were sunk on the course of this remarkable adit system whose total length was three and a half miles." Most of these mines had passed their peak of production by 1850; a few of them have been looked at again in the 20th century but not developed on a large scale. Gurlyn Mine produced some tin in 1904. Writing about Penberthy Crofts, Jenkin says, "in 1905 during a brief trial of the property, above adit, an underground water-wheel of large dimensions was found in perfect condition in the 22 fathom level from surface west of Daw's Shaft - where presumably it still remains." *(Mines and Miners of Cornwall,* Vol. XI)

CARBIS MILL

Carbis Mill was built for the stamping of tin during the 17th century; later it was used for fulling or tucking (cleaning new woollen cloth), and finally for grinding corn. D.E. Benney in *Cornish Watermills* states that the last miller died in 1941, "after which the mill was kept working by his widow." (Why, then, does she not qualify as "the last miller", I wonder.) The two waterwheels were removed about 1960; they and the overhead launder which fed them are shown in a photograph in Benney's book (page 55). "Also at this mill," he adds, "was the *Giant's Jump,* believed to have been the bedstone of a very ancient Cornish stamps, and consisting of two depressions in a corner stone between the two waterwheels, as if someone had pressed two footballs into the granite." The name, from the nearby Carbows Farm, means "paved road or causeway".

watercourse) runs close to the left side of the path before emptying into the river close to the mill buildings. This is not the millstream, which reached the mill at a higher level, but the "long tail or trench" which was dug to carry the water from the Deep Adit of Penberthy Crofts Mine: see Hamilton Jenkin: *Mines and Miners of Cornwall,* Vol. XI, page 17. After a further half-mile or so of pleasant riverside walking, with Trencrom on the skyline ahead, you reach a weir-cum-footbridge, with a larger bridge beyond.

8 *At this point you could go straight on for the quickest way back to the church - and it is an interesting walk, with various signs of old ponds and* *leats near Battery Mill (*). There are attractive views of St Erth church reflected in the reedy ponds created by the recovery of alluvial tin during World War 2: see the note on the River Hayle.* But for the full walk, turn left at the main bridge, over a cattle grid and up the farm road to Trewinnard.

BATTERY MILL

This was built by 1781 as a copper-rolling mill by the Cornish Copper Company of Copperhouse, Hayle; it was powered by five waterwheels. One of the uses to which the copper sheets were put during the Napoleonic Wars was to sheathe the bottoms of wooden naval ships, which were being attacked by Teredo worms. By 1873 the mill was owned "by one Gilbert who specialised in the manufacture of Cornish shovels of iron faced with steel, the furnaces being driven by a waterwheel that has long since disappeared." (The quotation is from *Industrial Archaeology of Cornwall* by Todd and Laws (1972). The Gilbert came from Phillack and so was presumably not related to the Gilberts of Tredrea Manor.) In 1972 Battery Mill was in use as a piggery, and by 1983 it was a mushroom farm. According to W.H.Pascoe, the C.C.C. called the mills at St Erth Battery Mills "because some copper vessels, notably those used for refining sugar, were known as Battery ware." *(The History of the Cornish Copper Company)*

TREWINNARD MANOR

"Trewinnard, the *Trewinedoi* of Domesday, has been without comparison the principal place in the parish." (Joseph Polsue: *Lake's Parochial History)* The family of the same name lived in the house probably before the Conquest; they were certainly there from at least 1372 (when a licence for chapels both here and at their other residence in Mawgan-in-Meneage was granted to them) till the reign of Elizabeth I. At that time Deiphobus Trewinnard was convicted of murder, and saved himself from execution by offering all his lands to one of the Queen's favourites, Sir Reginald Mohun. He duly assumed possession of the estate. In later years it passed through the hands of several other families, notably the Hawkinses, who also owned Trewithen (Probus) and much land at Pentewan, where Sir Christopher Hawkins (d. 1829) was largely responsible for the building of the harbour and mineral railway. The 1859 edition of *Murray's Handbook for Devon and Cornwall* states, "Some of the tapestry remains in this old house, and at the stables the rickety ruin of a gilded coach of primitive construction, which, it is said, caused no little ferment among the natives when it appeared with its four coal-black steeds at the churchyard gate of St Erth, as it was the first carriage introduced into the county." The Trewinnard Coach is still to be seen in the Royal Cornwall Museum in Truro, and a tapestry from the old house still hangs in the Trewinnard Chapel in the church. Writing in the late 1860s, Polsue lamented that "Trewinnard house has been so much altered latterly as scarcely to leave a trace of what it had been in former times." Be that as it may, it still looks a very fine residence, surrounded by productive land in a beautiful setting. It is now the home of Sir John and Lady Nott.

Soon you pass Trewinnard Mill with its barn housing "silly goats". It is rather surprising to find a mill so high above the river, but Polsue in *Lake's Parochial History* states, "The old mansion (Trewinnard) and grounds had the advantage of a stream of water, brought with great art over very uneven ground from a distance of two or three miles, conducted into almost every field, and supplying the house." It worked the mill, too, I suppose. Continue uphill on the path ahead. The goats were in the field beside the path when we were here, justifying the adjective on the barn by feasting on dry twigs. On that March day the fields all around Trewinnard Manor (*) were a mass of daffodils. The rather muddy track passed the outbuildings where flowers were being packed in boxes. After the right-hand bend you see St Erth church ahead and get a glimpse of Hayle Towans and the sea. Turn left, following the road.

9 After about a quarter of a mile, just after a left bend, take the treelined track on the right, going slightly downhill towards the village. Keep right where the paths divide, past a metal gate, and soon you reach Tredrea Manor (*). Go through the second gap on the right, opposite the house, and walk by the hedge on your right. Cross the stile at the corner and go straight on towards the village. After a stone cattle-grid you pass between houses and reach the road. Public toilets are on the right here. Turn right, crossing the ancient four-arched bridge which spans a flood-prevention overflow

TREDREA MANOR

The present occupant of Tredrea, Doris Harry, told us the house dates from the 17th century, and that the low hipped roof is now the only part of the original roof remaining. (According to *Lake's Parochial History,* the old house was "taken down" in 1750.) Tredrea is, Ms Harry said, the only manor on the estates of Lord St Levan. Early in the 18th century the lease passed by marriage to John Davies of Bosence (near Relubbus), whose daughter Catherine married the curate of St Erth, Edward Giddy. The reason for telling you all this is that their son, Davies Giddy, was one of the most remarkable Cornishmen of his period (1767-1839). He is better known as Davies Gilbert (he adopted his wife's maiden name when he married at the age of 50), but even that name hardly commands instant recognition, because - to borrow the title of a book about him - he always preferred to be "beyond the blaze" of publicity. Nicknamed "The Cornish Philosopher", after a distinguished career at Oxford he trained as a surgeon but devoted much of his time to the study of science, especially botany and geology. He was an M.P. for thirty years, representing Bodmin for most of that time, and he became President of the Royal Society. The breadth of his interests can be gauged by the fact that his many publications included a book of Cornish Carols and Melodies and a parochial history of Cornwall. It was Davies Gilbert who selected Brunel's design for the Clifton Bridge, and who encouraged and promoted the work of Humphry Davy, Richard Trevithick and Goldsworthy Gurney, the inventor of numerous devices such as the steam jet used by Stephenson in the "Rocket". Polsue sums up Gilbert as "a gentleman distinguished by his affability of manners, scientific knowledge, and talents as a statesman."

channel as well as the river itself, and soon you are back at the old Georgian school building and the church. The Star Inn, said to date from 1686, is a short way up the village street, which unfortunately lacks pavements so needs to be walked with care. A safer but longer route to the pub is mentioned in point 1 (lines 20-21). Among many points of interest in the village is Mena House, next to the Star and reputed to be even older; it was once a coaching-house called the New Inn. Notice also Churchtown Cross, opposite the pub. It is described in detail by A.C.Langdon in *Old Cornish Crosses* (1896), being, he says, "entirely different from any other in the county, owing principally to the remarkable shape of the head." Shortly before Langdon published his book the cross had been "with some ceremony, handed over by Lord St Levan to the care of the good folk of St Erth."

WALK 6
GWINEAR AND ANGARRACK
plus brief details of a walk through the old mining area south of Gwinear

Each walk is a little under three miles .

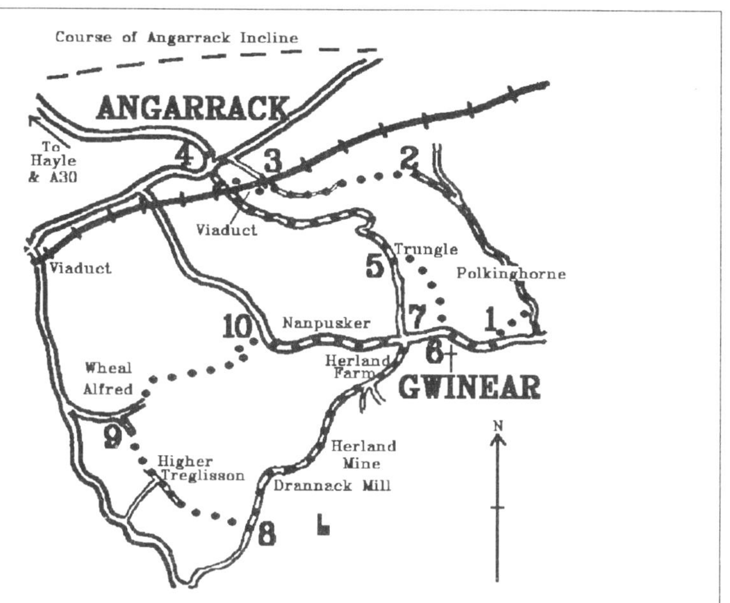

The main walk links an ancient parish church and an attractive village of great historical interest. The route is along farm tracks and field paths, and about half of it runs through the pretty valley of the Angarrack Stream or one of its tributaries. The fact that both Gwinear and Angarrack have a pleasant pub helps to make this an ideal gentle amble for a morning or afternoon. The countryside through which the other walk passes is almost as enjoyable; the big areas of "burrows" or waste heaps may spoil it for some, but equally they will be a special attraction for those who want to learn more about some of the oldest and richest mines in West Cornwall. Unfortunately, part of the Wheal Alfred set is now used as a public tip, and the walk route skirts this, but only for a few yards. The main reason why I am giving only a qualified recommendation to this walk is that one section of the path - about half a mile - was in need of attention when we walked it: parts were somewhat overgrown, though not enough to present serious problems in March, and several stiles were in a bad state or had vanished completely so that walls had to be clambered over. However, notices were on display indicating that various tracks and paths in this area are due to be upgraded, so I have hopes that things will improve. Gwinear has an unusually active and effective Footpaths and Bridleways Association, but this section of the route is in Hayle Parish. Both walks included a good many muddy patches in late spring.

GWINEAR

The small mining village, its grey granite terraced cottages strung out beside the road, seems to be in a different world from the ancient church, dedicated to the Irish prince who is said to have led the party of Celtic "saints" that landed at Hayle about 500 AD. (See the note on Riviere in Walk 7.) A few fragments of a Norman church remain, and the chancel includes 13th century work, but the tower and most of the rest of the building date from the 15th century. The old pews, along with much else, were taken out during the Victorian restoration (1881), but some of the Jacobean bench-ends were used to make the pulpit and litany desk. The tower has a lantern turret, in which it is said fires were once lit as a guide to seafarers. Inside the church is a wall tablet to one of the Lanyon family (said with the stress on the second syllable), another member of which achieved at least local fame by having sailed the world with Captain Cook. Lanyon Farm is a little to the north-east, and is not to be confused with the Lanyon in Morvah, Penwith. (See Sheila Bird's *The Book of Cornish Villages,* page 44.) Perhaps the most interesting grave in the churchyard is that of John Harvey, who established the great iron foundry at Hayle. That is on your right as you enter by the main door; but don't miss the headstone on your left at the same point, dedicated to Henry Hendra: "He was an honest, sober and industrious miner, whose constant attendance within these sacred walls, at the hours of public worship, procured him the distinguishing epithet of *THE CHURCHMAN.*" He died at the age of 35. Also in the churchyard are several ancient crosses; the two close to the main path both have drilled holes, suggesting that they were used as gateposts before being moved here. The larger one was brought from about half a mile away in 1858, and the smaller from Polmenor Downs, north of Carnhell Green, in 1984.

Directions are given from Gwinear (*). Probably the easiest way to drive there is to take the turning signposted Angarrack from the big roundabout on the A30 at the eastern edge of Hayle. At the crossroads in Angarrack turn right, then at the next juction sharp left. The best place for parking, certainly if you are doing the walk to Angarrack, is at the Church Hall, which is on the left just after you have passed the Royal Standard Inn. Although a notice there forbids unauthorised parking, Mr W.Tregenza, Chairman of the Association mentioned in the introductory note, assures me that walkers are considered to be very much authorised! For the other walk you could avoid about half a mile on the road by parking near Herland Farm, which is the last farm before you reach the church. A small layby on the left usually has space for a couple of cars. The directions for that walk start at the end of point 6.

1 The path is signposted and begins at the back of the Church Hall (formerly the village school). It runs in front of a row of terraced cottages, crosses a cattle grid and then goes straight on across a field. After the next grid turn left on the drive to Polkinghorne Manor. Though not shown on the maps as a right of way, this has recently been dedicated as a public byway by the owner, Mr Henry Laity. It makes an attractive walk: the high banks were thick with primroses in April, and on the far side of the extensive buildings of Polkinghorne it is lined with trees. When you cross the stream you may notice a small building on the right with a corrugated roof: this contains what the OS map names as a Hydraulic Ram, "a device," states my dictionary, "whereby the pressure head produced when a moving column of water is brought to rest is caused to deliver some of the water under pressure." (Got that?) Next bear left, following the yellow arrow on a white circle.

2 After going through the farm gate turn left and head for a group of derelict farm buildings. Go through the gap between two of them, then keep beside the hedge on your right till you reach a stone stile. (This area, by the way, is one of many places both in and out of Cornwall called Coldharbour, a place-name I have never seen explained. There is another just south-east of Towednack.) Cross the stile and then walk beside the hedge on your left for a few yards. After that continue at about the same level above the valley, crossing a rough stone stile on the left of a farm gate. This pleasant grassy lane runs gently downhill past a small quarry, perhaps opened specifically to provide building stone for Mellanoweth Farm, which comes a few yards later. The name means "new mill", and we were told by a local gentleman that the farmer used to grind his corn with the aid of a waterwheel some 15ft. in diameter. John Higgans, writing in *Old Cornwall,* suggests that there may have been a tin-stamping mill on this site. Now the lane becomes a minor road among houses on the edge of Angarrack. The name means "the rock" - compare Carrick Roads, in the Fal Estuary, named from "Black Rock".

3 Immediately before the viaduct (*) take the path down on your left, which leads you under the viaduct at ground level and then winds among houses, crossing the Angarrack Stream (or River) beside a road. Turn left on that, picking up the directions at point 4, to return to Gwinear, but if you want to have a look at Angarrack and/or visit the pub turn right. Notice that the small group of new houses on the left as you approach the crossroads has

ANGARRACK VIADUCT

As explained in the note on the Hayle Railway (Walk 7), the West Cornwall Railway changed the route in 1852. In order to avoid the steep incline at Angarrack they built a viaduct 266 yards long and 100 ft. high, using stone piers and a timber superstructure. It was replaced by the existing viaduct under the ownership of the Great Western Railway. The work took three years, 1883-5, and evidently it was a period of some turbulence for the village, with labour disputes and more than one fatal accident. Donald Bray in *Stories of the North Cornish Coast* imagines the scene:

Stonemasons hammer, 'midst the busy din
Chisel the granite; blocks squeal, scaffolds soar;
Pier beyond pier, arch beside arch, begin
To rival the proud aqueducts of Rome.

been named "Vellan Parc", that is "Mill Field" ("vellan" and "wellen" are alternative forms of the Cornish word *melin,* a mill): this refers to the main watermill of the village, called Angarrack Mill or Mellenvrane, "Crow Mill" or "Mill by the Rookery". Documents show that there was a mill on this site by 1343; it was rebuilt in three storeys in 1852, but closed down in or about 1874 as a result of the great enlargement and modernisation of Loggans Mill, on the eastern edge of Hayle, which was owned by the same man. The mill was eventually demolished during the 1980s to make way for this development. Several other names perpetuate the memory of the fine old building: the houses at the crossroads are named Mill House and Mill Brook, and the road ahead is called Grist Lane. If you go a short way up there, past the village pump, you will come to the site of the Angarrack Smelting House (*), which is now transformed into Angarrack Mews: the date "1706" over one door indicates the oldest part. Mr Mike Hunt told us that the typical smelting-house ventilation roof survived until the rebuilding in 1988. Donald Bray in *Stories of the North Cornish Coast* states that in 1692 a tin-stamping mill was set up "next door" at Hillside; looking at the rather imposing house which is now the Hillside Hotel, we wondered if that was originally the smelting-house manager's residence. Back at the crossroads, turning left up Hatch's Hill will take you to the Angarrack Inn. We haven't visited it, but both its food and its beer have been enthusiastically

ANGARRACK SMELTING HOUSE

Until the end of the 17th century tin was smelted in "blowing houses", where bellows were used to raise the temperature in blast furnaces fuelled by wood and charcoal, but in 1702 Robert Lydall took out a patent for a "reverberatory furnace" which made use of coal and anthracite. Soon afterwards, despite much opposition from those with a vested interest in the old method, a smelting house using ten of the new furnaces was set up at Newham, Truro, by Lydall in partnership with the aptly-named Francis Moult. In 1704 Francis Moult & Co. established another such smelter, with six furnaces, at Angarrack. It seems to have had a long and successful career, not closing until 1881.

recommended to us by several locals. The name of the road after it crosses the stream is Steamers Hill. This presumably refers to the stationary steam engine which hauled trucks up the Angarrack Incline, and perhaps also to the locomotives: see the note about the Hayle Railway in Walk 7. (Kenneth Brown tells me that Steamers Hill is actually the railway incline itself, and is so shown on old maps: the name should not have been applied to the road.) The top of the incline was at or very near the point where the railway track crossed the road, about half a mile up from the pub. Most of the engine house at Angarrack was destroyed by a fire in 1847, though the engine itself was little damaged, and the rope for hauling was saved. (See Cyril Noall's *Cornish Mine Disasters.)*

4 To complete the walk, return the same way at first, turning left at the crossroads (Riverside), but going straight on under the viaduct, beside the stream with its many little bridges and two or three small weirs. Just beyond the entrance to Mellanoweth Farm continue ahead over one of the two streams that meet here. Soon the path or track winds uphill among the buildings of Trungle Mill Farm. The mill itself must presumably have been down in the valley, since John Higgans states that it was "demolished in 1987 to make way for a housing development." Built as a corn mill before 1754, it was taken over by W.Hosken & Sons of Loggans Mill (the big derelict mill building still - for the time being - dominating the entrance to Hayle from the A30 roundabout on the east side) and used to crush bones for fertilisers. In 1895 it had two waterwheels, so arranged that the water could be switched from one to the other to drive different grindstones. Some copper and lead mining was carried out in this part of the valley: small mines called Mellanoweth (Wheal Maggot), Cold Harbour and Trungle worked from about 1808 to 1810. Little if any trace remains of them now on surface, but the Pathfinder map does indicate tips east and south of Trungle Farm, whose name means "farm of the mine-working" (Cornish, "tre-mongleth") according to Oliver Padel, although Mr Bertram Squire, who lives there, explains it as "homestead near the church" (tre(n)-eglos"). A leaflet available in the church mentions that "the site of the original celtic church is claimed to be at Trungle." On the way up to Trungle Farm the track - becoming increasingly muddy - passes close to a field where Roman silver and copper coins were found in about 1850. A gate on the right affords a good view of Angarrack with the towans and the houses of Carbis Bay beyond, below the steeple-like Knill's Monument; further left is Trencrom.

5 Just after going through the gate leading to Trungle Farm, cross the stile on your left and follow the hedge on your right. If the conditions are clear enough you will see Carn Brea on the skyline to the left now, crowned with the de Dunstanville Monument. Don't go through the gap, but turn right at the first corner and head towards the church, still with the hedge on your right. Cross a stile, and at the end of the next field go a few yards left over a stone cattle-grid before continuing towards the church. Another cattle-grid brings you to the road.

6 Turn left for the church, Gwinear village and the Church Hall.

A ROUND WALK ON THE SOUTH SIDE OF GWINEAR

7 From the suggested parking place near Herland ("long pool") Farm, walk through the farmyard (Drannack Lane). Soon there are good views to the right of the Angarrack viaduct and the sea, with Carbis Bay and St Ives in the distance. Keep to the main track as it curves gently right, downhill through the area known locally as "The Burrows", where there are old shafts and big waste tips all round, on both sides of the valley - remains of Herland Mine (*). Continue down to Drannack ("spinney") Mill, an old manor mill which finally ceased working in the 1930s. At the bridge, look left to see the new-looking pond and the ruined engine house of "Wheal Drunk", properly South Alfred Mine (*). Now the track or byroad runs uphill past ruined cottages.

HERLAND MINE

This ancient mine was already producing copper early in the 18th century, and by 1746 was employing a 70in. Newcomen engine. William Borlase described Herland as one of Cornwall's "first and greatest copper mines". Most of the small enterprises that had been working this area amalgamated in 1791 and bought a 63in. engine from Chacewater Mine; by 1794 another engine (this one a 60in. model of a novel design introduced by "Ned" Bull: see the note on Halamanning, Walk 4) was also at work trying to overcome the severe problems of underground water that plagued Herland. By 1796 the prospects for the mine looked bleak, partly because of legal proceedings brought by Boulton and Watt against Bull for infringing their patent; but two years later great excitement was caused by the discovery of rich deposits of silver. This brought in some £8,000, but that had to be set against losses of over £19,000 during the period 1792-8. The mine closed in 1807 but by 1815 was operating again, and great expense was being lavished on it. Another engine of novel design was erected, this time by one Richard Trevithick. (This 33in. pole engine is, Kenneth Brown tells me, "splendidly described in Dickinson & Titley's *Life of Richard Trevithick*.") Largely through inept management, the mine closed again before the end of 1816. A further period of activity, from 1823 to 1843, was much better organised, with two 80in. engines set to work in November 1823, but the mining historians appear to disagree about the financial outcome: Trounson refers to profits of £90,000 and Jenkin to considerable losses. From 1854-74 Herland worked again in conjunction with Rosewarne Mine.

SOUTH ALFRED MINE

An old mine called Bandowers, which had closed before 1819, was reopened as South Alfred for a few years during the 1860s. It seems to have met with little success - its only recorded sales were of copper to the value of £7 - so it is rather ironic that the engine house built for its 45in. pumping engine still stands, whereas no building from the much greater mines hereabouts has survived. The nickname, "Wheal Drunk", may be a clue to the mine's failure, since it is supposed to refer to the mine captains' fondness for the bottle.

8 Near the top, cross the stile on your right. It is rather awkward to climb, as is the next one, on the opposite side of the field. The field beyond that had been planted and the path not reinstated when we were there, and instead of a stile at the next boundary there was a rough wall to climb, with barbed wire on the far side. From here there is a good view to the right, embracing St Agnes Beacon, Carn Brea and the engine house of South Condurrow on the skyline to the right of it. After another wall - rather rickety - the path runs between hedges and was somewhat overgrown, but then came a clearer section and a view of the sea and St Ives. Continue ahead through two metal gates at Higher Treglisson farm, and later through the most dilapidated wooden gate I have ever seen - if it's still there. Soon you pass the large greenhouses and attractive Georgian-looking house at Lower Treglisson and come to a road.

9 Turn right, then take the track on the left, passing the sign announcing that Wheal Alfred (*), whose dumps cover a large area to the left, is a "Site of Special Scientific Interest", though to us it looked like the local rubbish tip. After the left curve, take the second track on the right, with a hedge on your right. To the left now is the small Guildford Viaduct. Keep to the wide track across a field, and after crossing the wooden bar at the top continue in roughly the same line, heading directly towards Carn Brea and a little to the left of the church tower. At the hedge turn left till you come to a stile on your right (steps down) after about 100 yards. Walk down beside the hedge on your right. At the end of the field there is a steep climb down to the road.

10 Turn right on that, down to Nanpusker Farm in the valley bottom, with its stream and pool, then uphill to Herland Farm and Gwinear.

WHEAL ALFRED

The early history of this copper mine has been described in great detail by A. K. Hamilton Jenkin (Journal of the Royal Institution of Cornwall, 1959), not only because it was the most important one in this district, but because the "Alfred" was his great-grandfather. Alfred's father, William Jenkin, conducted a vigorous correspondence, much of it concerned with mines round Hayle and Gwinear, and his letters written between 1790 and 1820 can be read in *News from Cornwall* (Westaway Books, 1955). The figures regarding Wheal Alfred's output, profit and loss are confused by the fact that several mines with similar names, such as Great Wheal Alfred, East Wheal Alfred and Wheal Alfred Consols, worked separately or in conjunction at different times. What does seem to be clear is that despite enormous output during the 18th and 19th centuries the shareholders sustained heavy losses on several occasions, and that all work on what Dines calls "this large but fluctuating sett" ceased in 1864. There was talk of reopening the mines in 1907 but nothing was done, and J.H.Trounson believed that was a wise decision; in *The Cornish Mineral Industry* he lists various factors which, he says, "combine to make any further reworking of these properties about as unattractive a speculation as anything that can be thought of in Cornwall."

WALK 7
PHILLACK AND THE TOWANS, plus a short walk around HAYLE

About 3.5 miles for the Phillack walk.
Exploring Hayle would add about 2 miles,
or nearly 3 if you walk out to Norwaymen's Wharf.

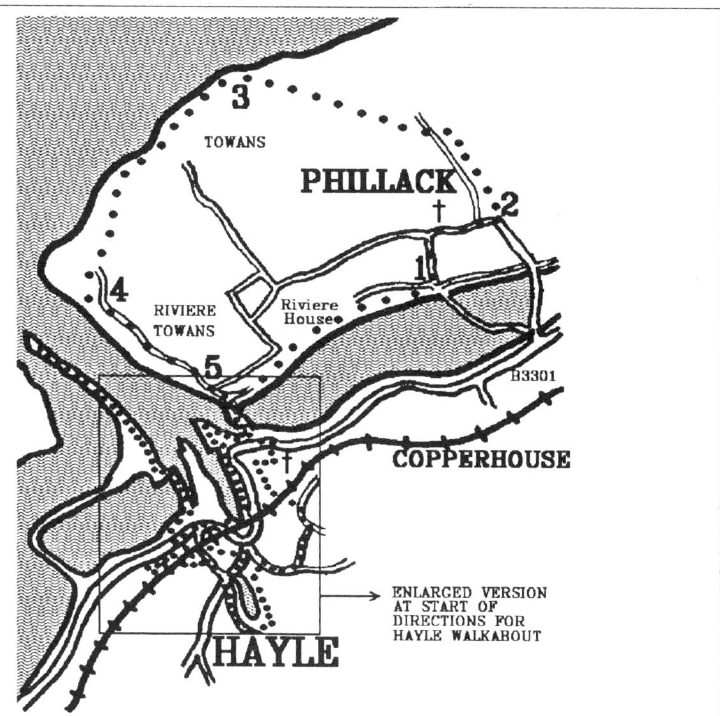

The Phillack walk is certainly one of contrasts, and it has to be admitted that the main contrast is between the magnificence of the natural scenery and the tatty or at worst hideous works of man scattered about over it. Luckily, there are some beautiful buildings too, such as the Godrevy lighthouse and the ancient churches of Phillack and Lelant, and the view of the long terraces of Copperhouse across Copperhouse Pool is, I think, both impressive and attractive. A very pleasant path has been developed on the Phillack side to take full advantage of that scene. An important compensation for the ugliness or at least dreariness of much else on the second half of the walk is the wealth of interest it contains for anyone wanting to understand the development of industry in Cornwall, and also for those with ideas about planning for the future. As for the scenery, it really is something special. After a relatively unspoilt stretch of dunes comes one of the finest stretches of beach in the country, bounded by two lovely islands: "The Island" at St Ives to the west, Godrevy Island with that beautiful lighthouse to the east; and a little later you have an equally fine

but very different view of the Hayle estuary. Despite a few steep slopes among the sandhills, it's an easy walk and unlikely to be muddy underfoot. An attractive and cosy old pub, luridly named The Bucket of Blood, is conveniently placed near the church, but you may have to go into Hayle for bar food, except during the season and sometimes at weekends in the winter. There are several cafés, beach shops and hotels that serve drinks and food among the holiday caravans and chalets on the western part of The Towans; all of these appear to be closed out of season, but a well-recommended pub, The Bluff, is, I believe, open all year round. For an account of part of this walk as experienced in 1870, read "Kilvert's Cornish Diary" (Alison Hodge, 1989), pages 32-8.
The walk around Hayle itself is an "optional extra" which could be tacked on to the Phillack route or done separately. In the latter case I would suggest you use the pay-and-display car park at Foundry Square (almost opposite the White Hart), starting the walk at point 10. The history of Hayle is so rich and complex that nearly everything you see on such a walkabout deserves comment, and to do the subject anything like justice a book of at least this size would need to be devoted exclusively to it. All I can attempt to do in practice is to point out some of the more noteworthy details that can still be seen; but in all honesty you're likely to find the experience pretty confusing and perhaps boring unless you do some homework, preferably beforehand, which would enable you to see how these things fit into a pattern. A great deal has been written about Hayle over the years, but unfortunately most of it is in books now out of print or articles in learned journals, so a visit to a library or second-hand bookshop might be necessary. For those who want in-depth studies, the obvious recommendations are Edmund Vale's "The Harveys of Hayle" (Barton, 1966) and W.H.Pascoe's "The History of the Cornish Copper Company" (Truran, 1981). More manageable for most people will be the excellent chapter about Hayle contributed by Edward Wigley to Todd and Laws' "Industrial Archaeology of Cornwall" (David and Charles, 1972), and "The Tale of a Town" in "Stories of the North Cornish Coast" by Donald Bray (Truran, 1983). See also Cyril Noall's "Book of Hayle".

Phillack is signposted from the main road that passes through the centre of Hayle (B3301). If you are approaching from the roundabout on the A30 on the eastern side of the town, the Phillack turning is on the right after about half a mile. A little roadside parking is usually available just past the church, but it is better to turn left opposite the church, down the narrow Phillack Hill. At the bottom of that is quite a large area for parking.

1 From there, return up Phillack Hill. Notice the rectangular black blocks which have been used decoratively on the house on the right near the top. These are known as scoria blocks (*), and you will see a good many more of them in both Phillack and Hayle. On your left at the corner behind a gate and at the bottom of a few steps is a small spring of water, said to be Phillack Holy Well, although W.H.Pascoe suspects that the water may have been diverted here from somewhere north of the church during the Victorian restoration. A local legend tells of the 18th-century squire of Trevassack Manor who washed his mangy dog at the Holy Well and was thereafter

SCORIA BLOCKS

The black slag which was the main waste material resulting from smelting copper was put to good use for road-building and moulded into "bricks" weighing about two cwt. each. They have proved to be very strong and durable. The wharf walls near the smelting works were constructed of them, as were the "Black Bridge" and many other walls and buildings. Whether or not they look attractive is debatable: perhaps they help give a rather sombre atmosphere to Hayle and Phillack. The word "scoria" is the Latin term for mining-waste, and it appears as a place-name, Scorrier, in the heart of the Redruth-St Day mining region.

THE BUCKET OF BLOOD

This was formerly called the New Inn, as might be expected of the pub reputed to be the oldest in the neighbourhood: some parts of the building are, it is claimed, 900 years old. W.H.Pascoe in his book on the Cornish Copper Company says it was probably "one of the New Inns licensed under Queen Elizabeth I"; John Higgans, writing in *Old Cornwall* (Spring 1988), suggests it probably began as an ale-house in the 17th century. He says the reason for the gruesome name it now bears is unknown. There is a tale, though, that on one occasion during the pub's early days, when the innkeeper drew up the bucket in his well he found it full of blood, and a horribly mutilated corpse was discovered. The nickname stuck, despite restoration of the original name during the 18th century. The pub is also known locally as "Top of the Knob."

cursed: first his son and then he died soon after, his family was reduced to poverty, and Trevassack is now a sorry ruin. The well itself, having been profaned, is said to have lost its sacred properties. Turn left along Churchtown Road if you are already in need of a visit to The Bucket of Blood (*), but for the walk turn right, past Phillack Church (*), and continue along the road as far as the right-hand bend.

2 There turn left, following the Public Footpath sign to the beach. It starts with a few steps and a steepish short climb up on to the sand dunes or

PHILLACK CHURCH

An early name for it was Egloshayle, "the church on the estuary": compare Wadebridge. The church has since the 13th century been dedicated to St Felicitas, "a Roman lady who gave her sons and then herself to the Christian faith" according to Arthur Mee, but in the 10th century the saint was named as "Felec". Felec is presumed to have been Celtic, but nothing is known about him or her. Charles Henderson suggested it might be St Piala, the sister of St Gwinear (Fingar) (see the notes on Riviere in this walk and Gwinear in Walk 6), and this idea is stated as definite fact by Charles Thomas in his Illustrated History of the church (1960); but although the words "Phillack" and "Piala" may look alike, one must bear in mind that the "Ph" spelling was an invention of the 16th century. (A similar change from F to Ph occurred at Philleigh: see *Around Mevagissey,* Walk 4.)* Professor Thomas puts forward evidence of a pre-Christian burial ground north of the church, and believes that a Christian community was already established here by about 400 AD. The main support for this is a small granite block above the south porch which bears the "Chi-Rho" symbol, representing the first two letters of "Christos" in the Greek alphabet, in a form typical of the later part of the Roman occupation of Britain; but no-one knows where this stone was found by the Victorian restorers who incorporated it in the rebuilt church. A few traces of the Norman church remain, including the font and part of the altar, but like most other old Cornish churches Phillack was greatly enlarged in the 15th century, when the tower and north aisle were added, and then drastically "restored" during the 19th. In fact it was almost totally rebuilt: industrialisation was pushing the local population up very rapidly, and a lot more accommodation was needed. This was done during the time of Frederick Hockin, the third in a remarkable sequence of four rector/ squires from the same family who held office at Phillack from 1763 to 1922. (His son Edmund is credited by Donald Bray with having "introduced Rugby football to the Cornish": see *Stories of the North Cornish Coast.)* The churchyard contains several ancient tomb slabs and crosses, including a tall wheel-headed cross probably dating from the 10th century. Beside the scoria-block wall of the old vestry stand an inscribed gravestone, possibly 7th century, and a cross, described by Thomas as "crude and frankly quite undateable", which was found nearby at Bodriggy, Copperhouse.

* In a note added in 1990 Professor Thomas acknowledges that "Piala was not the original patroness."

"towans". Don't go down to the tarmacked drive on the left, which leads to the "holiday park" overlooking the beach. There is a confusingly large choice of narrow paths through the dunes, but you won't go far wrong so long as you keep the drive fairly close on your left. You can now see over Phillack church tower to Lelant Saltings, with Trencrom the most prominent hill on the skyline. Almost hidden by it is Trink Hill, and further right is Rosewall Hill, beyond St Ives. When you come to the Public Footpath signs, go left, crossing the holiday park drive. Keep to the main grassy track. Now the view opens up to include St Ives; further left is Carbis Bay, with Knill's Monument like a small spire on the hill above. Unfortunately, from this angle the scene is dominated by electricity poles, pylons and cables - probably a reflection of the fact that till quite recently there was a power station just down below. Continue towards the sea, passing under the main line of pylon-supported cables. It's rather like walking across a natural golf-course here, with holes designed to twist ankles rather than receive little white balls. Here or nearby there used to be a mine called Wheal Lucy (*).

WHEAL LUCY

Until 1871 there were a few old tin-workings on this site, but the new owner of the Riviere Estate, Canon Hockin, Rector of Phillack, quickly formed a new company, renamed the mine after his daughter Lucy, and spent what for the time was a vast sum of money equipping it with modern dressing floors and the latest machinery. This included the first set of Husband patent pneumatic stamps in Cornwall, making the little mine a showpiece. In an interesting article about Riviere House in *Old Cornwall,* Autumn 1980, B.J.Sullivan tells that a tunnel was driven direct from the mine workings to the front door of the house for the benefit of the mine manager who was living there. The venture was short-lived, however, despite a rich discovery of silver at a shallow level: it closed in 1874, having yielded tin to the value of about a quarter of the initial capital outlay. Another attempt to work it in the 1890s, when tin prices were at a low ebb, resulted in further losses. Cyril Noall gives a detailed history of the mine in *The St Ives Mining District,* and includes a photograph of the engine house (after it had been partly demolished to house smaller machinery) and other mine buildings. Two houses and the former post office on the Towans here were mine buildings, and no fewer than three adits emerged on the beach below, still visible if you know where to look. The engine shaft near the cliff edge was capped early in 1992.

3 When we arrived on Black Cliff above the beach I found the temptation to career down the sandy slope like some March lambkin irresistible, in spite of the fact that the resemblance between me and a lambkin would normally be hard to detect. It *was* March, however. I enjoyed the run but came to regret my rashness, because the sand on the beach is not quite firm enough to make for comfortable walking, and the task of climbing back up the slope turned the lambkin into a lumbering hippo. Walking up a down-escalator is another image that came to mind. In any case, you probably wouldn't get round the headland on the beach at high tide, and the views are best at the top. All in all, then, I suggest you stay up there: turn left and keep to the cliff edge, passing a war-time "pill-box". The view you soon get of the entrance to Hayle harbour shows very graphically the problems and indeed dangers of using it. It's not long, for example, since two experienced local fishermen were drowned when their boat was turned over on the sand-bar which has re-formed now that the two sluicing-ponds are no longer in use. The coast path runs among holiday homes, hotels, beach shops, cafés and assorted tumbledown shacks which appear to be full-time dwellings. Man has done his utmost to spoil this beautiful place, but not, I'm pleased to say, with complete success. Keep heading towards the tower of Lelant Church; a few acorn signs help you to keep to the official coast path. When you reach the shore at the mouth of the estuary you have a good view of a long, rather black spit separating the two channels (the Hayle River on the far side and the Angarrack River on the near side); this was once the site of Norwaymen's Wharf (*). Below Lelant Church (now surrounded by a golf course, but once there were houses around the church) is Lelant Quay.

Lelant and Norwaymen's Wharf as seen from the Phillack side

NORWAYMEN'S WHARF

Its name, often given as Norwayman's Dock or Quay, refers to the Scandinavian ships which once regularly called with cargoes of timber. The shallowness of Hayle harbour meant that large ships had to dock here near the mouth of the estuary. Much of the timber was required by the smelting works at Copperhouse, and the usual procedure was to float it there in the form of rafts.

4 We walked back towards Hayle on the dirt road; the foreshore would probably have made pleasanter walking, but at least we could see rather more at the higher level - for example, on our left the site of what was once Cornwall's only National Grid power station, built in 1910 and closed down in 1977. The building was demolished about 1981. During World War 2 a chemical plant opened beside the power station. Its main business at first was obtaining magnesium from sea water, but later it turned to the production of bromine to prevent "knocking" in petrol engines. The chemical factory made use of waste heat from the power station. Toxic effluent from the chemical plant killed all the marine life in Copperhouse Pool, and it is only within the last ten years that birdlife has returned there. The old stack is all that remains of the only glassworks in the county (1917-25). The disused quarry housed the Hayle Lifeboat from 1866 until that service finished in 1920; later there was an Esso oil depot there. The sandhills above are Riviere (*) Towans. We continued along North Quay,

RIVIERE

Just west of Phillack Church is Riviere Farm, and the sandhills just west of that are known as Riviere Towans. Although the name, locally pronounced "Rovier", looks as if it means "river", and some scholars say that indeed it does, the interpretation "Great King" (from Cornish, *roy veor)* is suggested by others, including W.H.Pascoe, whose book *Teudar, A King of Cornwall* (1985) is the most detailed investigation I have come across of the history and/or legends surrounding this area. In 1537 John Leland reported that "Revier castle" was "almost at the east part of the mouth of the River Hayle, now as some think drowned with sand." Pascoe argues that the Riviere estate could originally have covered a large area, stretching from the estuary eastwards at least as far as the church, and he considers three possible sites of the "castle" itself, finally concluding that the most likely place is just north of the present church building, in an area where evidence of Iron Age and very early Christian burials has been found beneath the ever-encroaching sand. This, then, may have been the principal castle of a "king" or chieftain living in the second half of the 6th century, whose territory seems to have extended as far south as the Lizard and as far east as Goodern, close to what is now Truro, where he is supposed to have had another castle. (See Walk 1 in *A Second View from Carn Marth.)* His name appears in various contexts as Tudor, Tewdwr, Tewdrig and Theodore, but the commonest form is Teudar. Legend portrays him as a cruel pagan tyrant whose most notorious deed was to mount a treacherous attack from the rear on a party of Irish Christians, "missionaries" or "saints". Another interpretation is that he was quite justifiably defending his kingdom against a gang of invaders, having probably already suffered from the incursions of Saxons on his southern shores. He might even have been a Christian: "Theodore" means "gift of God". 777 of the Irish are said to have arrived at Hayle together and then split into two groups; the ones who went south reached the safe strongholds of Tregonning and Godolphin Hills, but many of those who headed east under the leadership of Prince Fingar (St Gwinear) were massacred.

formerly the coal-wharf; it is now occupied by a car spares business and therefore probably out of bounds, although nobody seemed to object to our presence. Keeping company with the rusty and rotting cars were several rusty and rotting boats, reminders - like the redundant railway lines - of the long-gone prosperity of Hayle as a port. Here and there among the comparatively modern rails with their wooden sleepers - remains of the GWR Hayle Wharves Branch - are some granite setts of the type found on the routes of other early mineral lines, such as the Portreath Tramway, the Redruth and Chasewater Railway - and the Tresavean Branch of the Hayle Railway (*), described in Walk 11 of *A Second View from Carn Marth.* The setts here, of course, are a relic of the Hayle Railway. Some of them were taken up and used to build a wall beside the nearby slipway. Follow the rails until you come almost to the swing bridge. *Now if you want to extend the walk into Hayle itself, continue ahead on the harbourside road and read the directions from point 5;* but to complete the three-and-a-half mile walk around Phillack turn left and walk along the north side of Copperhouse (*) Pool. Running the whole length of it and following the course of the original Hayle Railway is the King George V Memorial Walk, sometimes known as the Coronation Walk, nicely laid out with bulbs and shrubs, a few palms, several small ponds, seats and public toilets. On the opposite shore at the start, near the swing bridge, is one of the oldest quays at Hayle, which was in use from about 1740 by a merchant called John Curnow and his partners. The facing of scoria blocks was added later, when it was used as a wharf by the Copperhouse company. Behind that is Hayle Church (*), and a few hundred yards further on is the Passmore Edwards Institute (*). Up on the left, though not easily seen from this angle, is Riviere House (*); and later, as you approach the causeway known as the Black Road (*) and the suggested parking place, notice the Georgian former alms-houses just left of the path, now extremely neglected and approaching the condition of some ecclesiastical ruin, despite the ancient television aerial at one end. You might care to walk on a little further along the former railway track to look at what is claimed to be Cornwall's oldest railway bridge (1835), crossing the Angarrack Stream. (There are older bridges on the Poldice Plateway and the Redruth and Chasewater Railway, so the claim depends on how you define "railway" and "tramway".)

The remaining "boxed notes" for the Phillack walk are on the following pages:

THE HAYLE WALKABOUT STARTS ON PAGE 69.

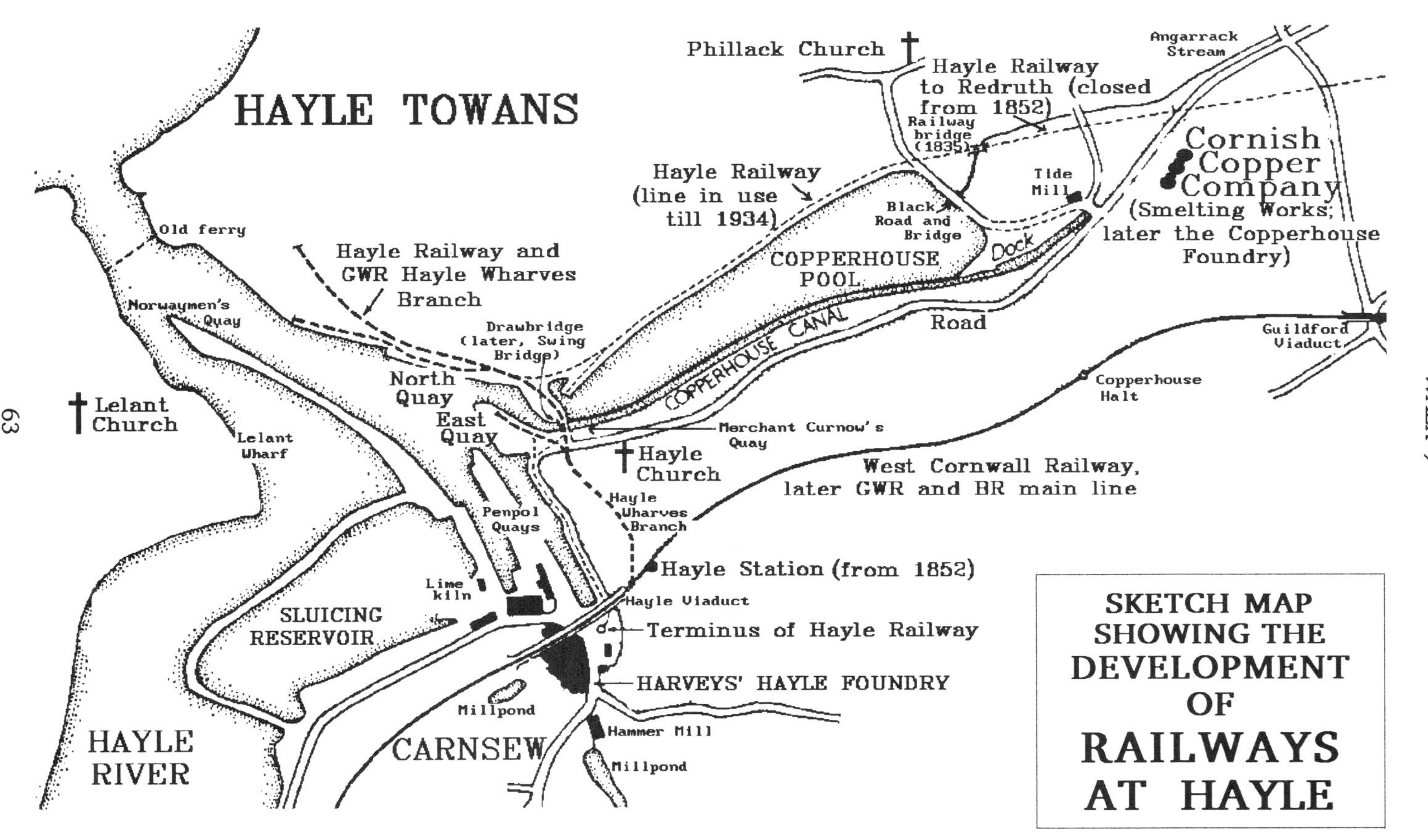
SKETCH MAP
SHOWING THE
DEVELOPMENT
OF
RAILWAYS
AT HAYLE
HAYLE TOWANS
Phillack Church
Hayle Railway
to Redruth (closed
from 1852)
Railway
bridge
(1835)
Angarrack
Stream
Cornish
Copper
Company
(Smelting Works;
later the Copperhouse
Foundry)
Tide
Mill
Hayle Railway
(line in use
till 1934)
Black
Road and
Bridge
COPPERHOUSE
POOL
Dock
COPPERHOUSE CANAL
Road
Guildford
Viaduct
Copperhouse
Halt
Old ferry
Hayle Railway and
GWR Hayle Wharves
Branch
Norwaymen's
Quay
Drawbridge
(later, Swing
Bridge)
North
Quay
East
Quay
Merchant Curnow's
Quay
Lelant
Church
Lelant
Wharf
Hayle
Church
West Cornwall Railway,
later GWR and BR main line
Hayle
Wharves
Branch
Penpol
Quays
Hayle Station (from 1852)
Lime
kiln
Hayle Viaduct
SLUICING
RESERVOIR
Terminus of Hayle Railway
HARVEYS' HAYLE FOUNDRY
Millpond
Hammer Mill
Millpond
HAYLE
RIVER
CARNSEW

THE HAYLE RAILWAY

The Hayle Railway opened in 1837-8, linking the ports of Hayle and Portreath to the important mining area around Camborne and Redruth, a total of just over 17 miles including several branches. The line was "standard gauge", 4ft. 8.5in. The first railway engine to be designed and made in Cornwall, the "Cornubia", was built for the Hayle Railway at the Copperhouse Foundry in 1838 (ten years after Stephenson's "Rocket"); it was described at the time as "a splendid piece of workmanship capable of 40 miles per hour." The line included several very steep sections or Inclines, and on the most severe of these, at Portreath and Angarrack, wagons had to be hauled up by ropes with the aid of stationary steam engines. Records exist of a hemp rope manufactured for this purpose in 1843, again by the Cornish Copper Company, which had its own Ropery, run at that period by a man called Mr Roper. It weighed about five tons, was 2,800ft. long and 10.5in. in circumference. (Incidentally, an 1836 Act of Parliament had specified the use of wire ropes on the Inclines, but Cyril Noall's account of the fire at the Angarrack engine house seems to confirm that hemp rope was used there. See *Cornish Mine Disasters.)* West of the Angarrack Incline, traces of which can still be seen on the north side of Angarrack village, the wagons were horse-drawn in the very early days, but later the locomotives were attached to the ropes on the Incline. The line ran along what is now the Memorial Walk on the north side of Copperhouse Pool to a terminus at the North Quay. The main terminus was at Harvey's Hayle Foundry, but for the line to reach that a drawbridge had to be built across the Copperhouse Canal, so as not to impede shipping using the old Copperhouse dock at Ventonleage. The line then crossed the Copperhouse wharf, formerly Merchant Curnow's Quay, and ran beside the Penpol River to the Foundry. Although the railway was built as a mineral line, from 1843 onwards passengers were also carried (according to a contemporary report "the closed carriages resembled the hold of a slave ship") and eight stations were built. Hayle Station was in Foundry Square, almost underneath the present viaduct. In 1846 the Hayle Railway was taken over by the new West Cornwall Railway and incorporated into a system linking Truro and Penzance. In 1852 the line was re-routed, avoiding the Angarrack Incline and keeping to the south side of Copperhouse Pool; and 14 years after that the West Cornwall Railway was in its turn absorbed by a larger concern, the Great Western. The line running on the north side of the Pool remained in use till 1934, and the one from Hayle Foundry along Penpol Terrace to North Quay was linked to the main line by means of the Hayle Wharves Branch, which continued in use until 1983. Until the 1960s the wagons on the old Hayle railway lines were hauled by horses. In 1877 the old drawbridge was replaced by a swing bridge which carried a road as well as the railway. Its hydraulic mechanism continued in full working order to the end, and can still be inspected.

COPPERHOUSE

Several small copper-smelting plants were set up during the late 17th and18th centuries in Cornwall (see Walk 6 in *Around St Austell* for an account of a very early one). One of the most successful was launched in 1754 at Carn Entral, south of Camborne, but the cost of transporting large amounts of coal by packhorse from Hayle prompted the partners to seek new premises close to the quays. In 1757 they leased land at Ventonleage (sometimes spelt "Ventonleague") beside the tidal pool then known as Est Loe and set up business as the Cornish Copper Company. Supplies of the scoria blocks described earlier were available free of charge to workers wishing to build their homes on the Company's land, and a new town that came to be called Copperhouse was thus created. ("The Copper House" was the nickname of a round chapel built in 1784 of slag blocks.) The vast quantities of slag that had to be dumped were put to use in creating new roads, embankments and quays; marshy land was reclaimed; in 1769 the course of the Angarrack Stream was canalised from Ventonleage westwards; and in 1788 a weir was built across the mouth of the Loe - by then known as Copperhouse Pool - so that with the aid of sluice gates tidal water could be trapped and then released an hour before low water in order to flush out some of the sand that was always threatening the port's access to the sea. Before that, no ship of more than 70 tons could enter the harbour, but by 1808 coal ships of 250 tons could reach the North Quay, and 120-ton vessels could use the smelting works quay at Ventonleage. Well before that time the Company had begun to diversify: early in the 1780s it bought up the quays at Penpol and with them the trade in mining merchandise that had been operated by "Merchant Curnow" and his partners. This was a wise move, because copper smelting in Cornwall was always doomed to failure in competition with South Wales ("fortunately for Cornwall", I am tempted to add, because its effects on the environment and the health of its workers were horrific): for every ton of copper ore smelted here, three or four tons of coal had to be shipped in. By 1790 a new threat to the Company's trade monopoly was emerging in the shape of Harvey's Foundry at Carnsew; the commercial battle that followed, sometimes called the Thirty Years' War, came to a head in the 1820s when the CCC ceased copper smelting and converted its buildings into a foundry in direct competition with Harvey's. The story is fascinating but too complex for a small book of walks to handle: see the books recommended earlier. Suffice it to say that after many successful years the Copperhouse Foundry (known in its later years as "Sandys, Carne & Vivian") closed in 1867 because of a severe slump in mining, and that all its land and assets were bought by the Harveys a few years later. The foundry buildings at Ventonleage were still apparently in fairly sound condition when photographed in 1963: see page 125 in Pascoe's book. Close by, one old industry has survived and is now the town's major employer, the engineering works of J. & F.Pool Ltd which was started nearly 150 years ago, specialising originally in sieves for use in the mines. When the old foundry was demolished in the 1970s, Pool's took over part of the site.

HAYLE CHURCH

The rapid growth of Hayle during the 19th century led to the creation of a new parish out of the western part of Phillack in 1870. It was named after St Elwyn, one of the group of Irish saints said to have landed at Hayle in the 6th century. Elwyn accompanied Breaca south up the Hayle River and escaped the fate most of the others met at the hands of Teudar: see the note on Riviere. The church (1886-8) was the last building created by J.D.Sedding, the designer of the Brompton Oratory. His restorations of many old churches in Cornwall are usually regarded as much more sensitive than most. Like All Saints, near the top of Killigrew Road in Falmouth, which Sedding completed just before this one, it is an impressive building, lofty and almost cathedral-like inside.

THE PASSMORE EDWARDS INSTITUTE

In *A View from St Agnes Beacon* I included a note about the Miners' and Mechanics' Institute in St Agnes, which was given to that village by John Passmore Edwards in the same year as the Hayle Institute was opened: 1893. Born at Blackwater just east of Scorrier in 1823, the son of a carpenter, he became involved in journalism in London, and after several loss-making ventures succeeded with *Building News;* later he bought the *Echo,* the first halfpenny newspaper. From 1880 to 1885 he was liberal M.P. for Salisbury. He twice refused a knighthood. He was a well-known champion of causes like Early Closing and Anti-Gambling, and as a pacifist he denounced the Crimean and Boer Wars. In his latter years he established many public libraries, hospitals, art galleries, technical schools and colleges, most but not all of them in his native county. The Institute at Hayle was equipped with a library and recreation rooms, but the aim was mainly to provide technological education: "to diffuse practical knowledge by practical means," in Passmore Edwards' own words. It was built on land given by Harvey's, and designed by Silvanus Trevail, who was to be jeered and pelted with eggs seven years later during the "Headland Riots" occasioned by his proposal to build the Headland Hotel in Newquay; he had already built the Atlantic. See *Around Newquay,* Walk 7.

RIVIERE HOUSE

Riviere House was built in 1791 by the Cornish Copper Company for John Edwards, who had been Manager since 1865. The roof is reputed to have been lined with copper sheets. In the cellars Edwards carried out scientific experiments, and it is said that this was the first laboratory ever visited by Humphry Davy, brought here by his patron Davies Giddy (Gilbert): see the note on Tredrea Manor in Walk 5. Isambard Kingdom Brunel stayed at Riviere House several times in 1840-2 while the Copperhouse Foundry was forging massive 24-foot chain links originally intended for the Clifton Suspension Bridge but actually used on the Royal Albert Bridge over the Tamar. Just before the Foundry was wound up in the late 1860s, the house was bought at auction by the Rector of Phillack, Frederick Hockin, who later acquired the whole of the Riviere Estate. He is said to have tiled the roof and sold off the copper sheeting for a handsome profit. The house had been renamed "La Rivière" and seems to have been in use as the rectory when Francis Kilvert visited the Hockins there in 1870. (See *Kilvert's Cornish Diary.*) For a few years shortly before World War I (everyone who mentions this seems to have a different account of the dates) the author Compton Mackenzie lived at Riviere House, and his autobiography has a description of it, including references to the "magnificent kitchen" and the cellars "like the crypt of a Gothic church." Mackenzie carried out an ambitious shrub-planting scheme, perhaps influenced by the current Rector of Ludgvan, A.T.Boscawen: see the note on Ludgvan Church in Walk 2. Its next occupant was a gentleman who proposed to carry out experiments on live animals there, whereupon he was asked to leave. (Apparently he then went to Acton Castle: see Walk 3.) After a period as a hotel, the house was commandeered during World War 2 for the Women's Land Army and later for British and American troops. Next it became a Youth Hostel, and this continued for at least 30 years, but it is now a private residence once more.

(My thanks to B.J.Sullivan for much of the above information: see the note on Wheal Lucy.)

THE BLACK ROAD AND BRIDGE and COPPERHOUSE MILL

The notes about scoria blocks and Copperhouse mention some of the uses to which the enormous quantities of black slag produced by copper smelting were put. In 1818 a road across the upper part of the pool, with a bridge over the Angarrack stream, was built of these materials to provide easy access from the works at Ventonleage to the Manager's house at Riviere and the North Quay. At the behest of the Rector of Phillack one of the two arches of the bridge was made high enough for him to pass under it in his boat on the way to and from his quay at the bottom of the Rectory garden: a neat illustration of the power and influence of the Hockin dynasty, even in its relatively early years. (See the notes on Phillack Church and Riviere House.) In about 1842 the Copperhouse Foundry decided to build a mill to grind grain as fodder for its horses. Since the Black Road had created a tidal upper pool, the obvious course was to build a tide-mill at the head of the canal: see the sketch map showing railway development. By impounding and then releasing the tidal water the Company was able to drive its mill and scour sand out of the canal at the same time. After 1862 the water power was supplemented by a steam engine. "Paddy's Mill" as it was called (Richard Paddy having been the first miller) was demolished in the late 1930s, and the stone from it was used in the construction of the Memorial Walk. The 40-foot stack and the engine house survived until the 1980s: despite an outcry from those who cared about Hayle's heritage, they were dynamited on 23rd July 1982.

The Black Bridge

HAYLE WALKABOUT

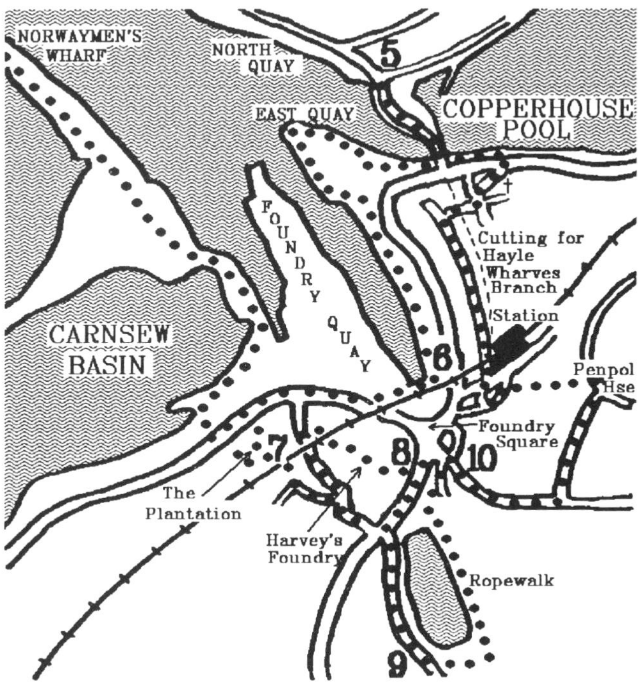

5 If you are doing this as part of the longer walk, continue ahead beside the harbour, as mentioned in the previous paragraph, passing on your left the Custom House (1862), which has a compass rose cut into its doorstep. It is now the Harbourmaster's Office. Pause here a moment and look across the harbour to Lelant church, then further right to the tip of Knill's Monument on the skyline; a little to the right of that and quite close to the shore on the Lelant side you may be able to make out the red-and-white box that houses video cameras, part of a system enabling the Harbourmaster to watch the harbour entrance. More details of this are given in Walk 8 (point 10). Cross the swing bridge, which originally carried the railway (Hayle Wharves Branch) on the left side. It was made at Harvey's Foundry and replaced the old drawbridge here in 1877. On the right at the start is the sluice gate controlling release of water from Copperhouse Pool; this, I am told, is now operated from South West Water's HQ in Exeter! Beyond that you will see the small engine-house and below it the gears and chains still intact, by which the swing bridge used to be opened and closed. On the far side, turn right on to East Quay, the building of which by the Cornish Copper Company in 1818 led to some of the most bitter enmity between that company and Harvey's. It is easy to see how it could be regarded as threatening access to the Penpol quays. In later years the Hayle Gas Company was based here, and some of its buildings remain (Taylor's Tyre Service occupies one), putting to shame most if not all of the more recent industrial buildings hereabouts. You can walk all round the edge of the quay, which gives a good view of the harbour, with Harvey's Foundry Quay (or Penpol Quay) close after you have rounded the seaward end. As you look south now towards Penpol Terrace it is obvious that the ground between that and the harbour is made-up land, with slag and other rubble piled on what was once the foreshore of the estuary. Continue past the Royal Standard Inn. This was once called the Passage House, since it was from here that travellers heading west would have had to start their low-tide crossing of the sands in the days before the building of the Hayle Causeway (1825). When Harvey's built their quay opposite (1819) they left an archway in it for the travellers to pass through. The archway was later blocked up, and when that section of the quay collapsed in the early 1960s it was rebuilt using metal piles. Continue ahead along the grassy path - the original trackbed of the Hayle Railway - among attractive flowerbeds opposite the houses of Penpol Terrace. Notice how the shops have been tacked on to the houses. This is a result of the former dominance of Harvey's in this area: the employees all had to use the Foundry's own emporium. Several of the shops retain interesting features of the late Victorian era and the early 20th century: notice, for example, the tiling on the Carnsew Gallery, originally a butcher's shop, and the date "1894" punched in holes under the doorstep of Biggleston's.

6 Immediately before the viaduct turn right. From this angle it is easy to see the curved or "scalloped" shape of the Foundry Quay wall, possibly designed to match the hulls of the ships that moored there, though it may have been the result of curves in the reef of rock on which the foundations are built. Continue along the main road (Carnsew Road, B3301, originally the A30) past Jewson's. Jewson's site and the surrounding area were formerly occupied by Harvey's shipyard and timberyard, plus buildings housing steam hammers and sawmills. *For a worthwhile extension continue until you come to a path on the right, signposted to "The Weir". This soon brings you to the side of Carnsew Basin, built by Harvey's during the 1830s as a sluicing pond to keep their own shipping channels clear of sand and silt. A fine pair of circular limekilns, probably dating from the 18th century, used to stand here. Edmund Vale's book (1966) has a photograph of them, and he comments that they "are more deserving than most of their kind of having a place in the Schedule of Ancient Monuments." They have vanished without noticeable trace. Go right and then left to walk out on to Norwaymen's Quay (see the earlier note), which gives excellent views of the harbour and estuary. On the way you will cross the entrance to the Basin, where a now derelict building once housed the sluice-gate mechanism. Return the same way - but if on the way back you cross the concrete bridge before turning right you will get a good view of the canal Harvey's built to serve the Foundry. Return to the road and turn left to continue the walkabout.* Cross the road and go up the steps to the King George VI Memorial Plantation. This is the site of an Iron Age cliff castle, built on the ideal site for watching over the estuary, one of the most important trade routes on the North Cornish coast. When Henry Harvey retired in 1844 he devoted much time to laying out pleasant gardens and walkways and building decorative arches here. If instead of going through the arch at the top of the steps you turn left and then climb the next flight of steps, you will find on your right an ancient memorial stone. The original lettering is now almost invisible, but the slate tablet above offers a translation of it. From here go up to the top of the Plantation, where a plaque

HARVEY'S HAYLE FOUNDRY

The story is often told, and it may be true, that Sir John St Aubyn of Clowance visited a blacksmith at Carnhell Green seeking a quick replacement for a lost shoe buckle. The smith promptly made the buckle from one of the gentleman's silver spoons, so impressing him that he urged the man to set up business on a larger scale at Carnsew. The smith was called John Harvey, and his move to Carnsew, which took place in 1779, resulted in the creation of the first and greatest of all Cornwall's iron foundries. His self-education in the techniques of casting; the success he and his descendants had in building their manufacturing and trading empire despite fierce and even violent opposition from the Copperhouse company; and the amazing feats of engineering they achieved - all these have been absorbingly described by Edmund Vale, and more briefly by several of the other writers I have mentioned. Some hints about what happened are scattered here and there in my own remarks, especially in the Hayle Walkabout directions and the note on Copperhouse. In the event, Harvey's final triumph over their greatest rivals was fairly short-lived: defeated by the declining fortunes of the mines, they closed the foundry and shipbuilding businesses in the early years of this century, though continuing as merchants into the 1980s.

The entrance to Harvey's Hayle Foundry. In the background are the curved walls surrounding what was the Foundry's vegetable garden.

gives details about the view, the history of the site and the discovery of the memorial stone - together with a (probably) more accurate translation of the inscription. The plaque refers to a Crimean War mortar manufactured by Harvey's. At the time of writing this was being cleaned and a new carriage was being made for it, but I understand that it will be on display again soon.

7 Now walk along the rough track or lane which crosses the main railway line. It leads down to the site of Harvey's Hayle Foundry (*). Opposite you when you reach the bottom of the lane are the derelict buildings of Foundry Farm. The main purpose of the farm was to provide horses and pack-mules for transportation of raw materials and of goods to customers. First it would be worth going a few yards to the right to see the impressive curved walls surrounding what was the Foundry's vegetable garden, and the entrance archway; but to continue the walk turn left - notice the brick arches in the building now occupied by Ford Spares - and go under the right-hand arch of the viaduct and through the small gap in the wall ahead. Turn right, back under the viaduct, at the first opportunity. Now you are at the heart of what has survived of the Foundry. On the right are the remains of one of the Pattern Stores. Ahead is the most impressive ruin, part of the Fitting Shop where engines were assembled - clearly in a dangerously derelict state and in urgent need of conservation. Down a side-passage to the left is a surprising survival, the old wooden drawing office, part of which is supported by two of the cast-iron pipes that were among the earliest products of the Foundry. They were used to carry water pumped up from the mines; before that, many Cornish mines had relied on hollowed-out tree trunks for the purpose! Go to the road (Foundry Hill) and turn left for a few yards, into Foundry Square. The large building on your left with an interesting roof-line, now called Foundry House, was the Cornubia Biscuit Factory. Opposite is the White Hart Hotel (1836); the little building attached to it on the far side was the original White Hart, built by Henry Harvey in 1824 for his sister Jane as a source of income for her when she was left as a grass widow by her famous engineer husband, Richard Trevithick. Barclays Bank was the emporium I mentioned earlier, and Lloyds was once the Foundry Market House. It was a two-storey building, and housed a cinema for a time, but suffered severe fire damage during the 1930s. The original Hayle Station, the terminus of the Hayle Railway, was in Foundry Square, almost underneath the viaduct built later by the West Cornwall Railway.

8 Now return along Foundry Hill. Until quite recently one of the most impressive relics of the foundry, another part of the Fitting Shop, stood on what is now an ugly, rubble-strewn patch of waste ground on the right side of the road: a row of tall arches affectionately nicknamed "The Coliseum". In 1983 a development company called Tekoa Hayle Ltd bought up much of the Foundry land and other parts of the harbour, and began preparing a

"The Coliseum" (part of the Fitting Shop of Harvey's Hayle Foundry) shortly before it's demolition. Photograph by Bill Newby.

The ruins of part of the Fitting Shop. The rough ground in front of it - a brilliant show of Valerian in June - is the site of "The Coliseum".

master plan for redevelopment of the port, but Tekoa's only lasting contribution to the history of Hayle appears to have been destruction of its heritage. The demolition of "The Coliseum" on 22 March 1984 is bitterly resented by many in the town. A local resident I met while researching this walk told me how she and many of her neighbours turned out at 8 am to try to halt the bulldozers. According to her, the only reason given for this act of vandalism was that a single stone from the old wall had fallen into the street. Soon on the left you will see the mill pond, created to provide power for industrial mills - more details later. Turn left along Millpond Avenue. Notice the attractive but small cottages at the start, built for the Foundry's workmen, and the much grander residences further along, with views over the pool, which housed the "white-collar" workers and directors of the company. At the end of this road a modern housing estate has been built on the site of the Mellanear Tin Smelting Works. This was started in 1837 by Williams Harvey & Co., who also owned the Trethellan smelter at Truro; it closed in 1905 but re-opened in 1915 as a result of the increased demand during wartime, finally ceasing operations in 1920. D.B.Barton in his *A History of Tin Mining and Smelting in Cornwall* quotes figures showing that between 1849 and 1861 Williams Harvey made far more profit from their two works than that earned by any contemporary Cornish tin mine. A photograph of the Mellanear works is on page 216 of his book.

9 Take the path on the left, cross the wooden footbridge, and walk along the recently restored Ropewalk. Notice the square iron slots in the wall on the left, and the circular and oblong pits on the right later - all relics of the rope-making process. Eventually you will pass through the restored remains of the hammermill, now called Millpond Gardens. A plaque on the wall near the far left-hand corner gives some information about the hammermill, boring mill and cornmill that once operated here. The cornmill is usually known as Trevithick's Mill because a son of Richard Trevithick managed it, and the Trevithick family remained in charge for most of its active life. It was originally intended to supply fodder for the foundry's horses; water power was not used for it, but at first a pony drove the stones, and in the 1830s when the mill was enlarged to produce flour for human consumption a steam-engine was substituted. In 1879 the mill building was further enlarged to five storeys and employed a beam engine of 180 h.p. Milling ceased during the 1890s, after which part of the building became a sweet factory, well known for its mint humbugs. Leave by the main archway and walk along the side road on the right, past the end of Tremeadow Terrace. This soon brings you back to Foundry Square, opposite the car park.

10 Turn right along Penpol Road (or, if you are starting the walk here, turn left on leaving the car park), and then left at Penpol Terrace. Continue to the top end, where stands one of Hayle's old manor houses, Penpol House. Lake's Parochial History records that "The family of Penpoll resided in the parish in 1577". The house and estate were bought by "Merchant Curnow" in the mid-18th century, and at his death in 1780 they passed to his son-in-law, Richard Oke Millett. Since Millett was a partner in the Cornish Copper Company, this greatly strengthened the Copperhouse company's hand in its struggle to monopolise trade at Hayle. Continue for a few yards along the road to the left, and take the path between walls on the left almost opposite Penmeneth House. This soon brings you to Hayle Station, where, as Brian Sullivan complained in his Hayle Town Trail (1983) "in recent years British Rail have destroyed almost every building of historic interest." Go a few yards to your left, through a gap on to the road, left again, then right on to a back-road or lane which passes under the railway. This gives quite a good view to the left, and on the right is the cutting that was dug for the Hayle Wharves Branch. Turn right and cross the wooden bridge over that. This brings you to Hayle Church (see the earlier note) - well worth a visit if you are lucky enough to find it unlocked. Go down to the main road, cross it (public toilets here), and turn left to cross the swing bridge, thus completing the Hayle Walkabout for those who incorporated it into the Phillack walk.

Of course, this route and my brief notes have scarcely scratched the surface of this fascinating place - even allowing for the fact that I have not included Copperhouse in it. For those who would like to explore more of the territory and learn more details I recommend Brian Sullivan's leaflet, mentioned above, even though a good deal has changed since he wrote it. Another cheap and handy source of information is the "Hayle - Perranporth Driveabout" published by the Cornwall Heritage Project in 1989. Both are available from the Copperhouse Book Centre, 26 Fore Street.

WALK 8
LELANT AND CARBIS BAY
with a possible extension to
KNILL'S MONUMENT AND HALSETOWN

About 8 miles, or it could be done as two walks of about 4 miles.

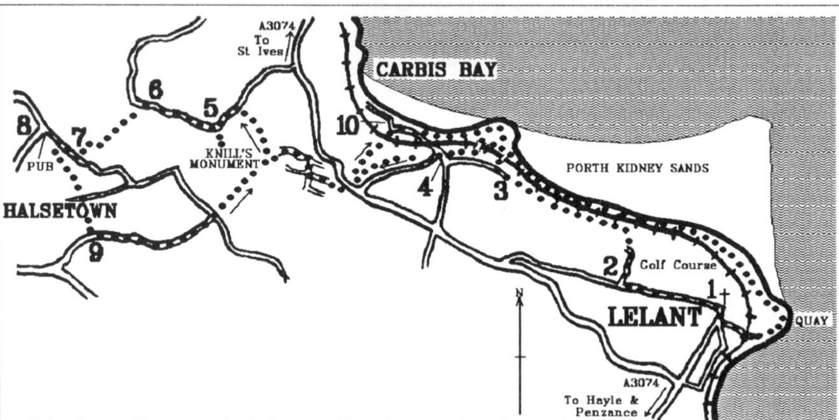

This is a figure-of-eight walk, the mid-point of which is at Carbis Bay railway station, so it splits neatly into coastal and inland halves, but is even better as an all-day ramble which is rich in historical interest and offers a great variety of wonderful scenery. Try to choose a clear day for it in order to benefit from the long views. It cannot really be called a tough walk, but it does include several quite long climbs. The most strenuous part is the more westerly section of the coast path; this comes near the end of the walk as I have described it, but you might prefer to "get it over with" at the start, in which case you could park at Carbis Bay (or get there by bus or train) and begin at point 10 in the directions. We had no particular trouble with mud on this walk, but were glad of sturdy boots. There are pubs at Lelant, Carbis Bay and Halsetown, but only the last of those is actually on the walk route; you do, however, pass a licensed restaurant at Carbis Bay where morning coffee, lunches and teas can be had, and shops where some provisions are available at Carbis Bay and Halsetown. The Polmanter Farm Tourist Park at Halsetown also has a shop. There are public toilets beside the walk route at Carbis Bay.

Lelant Church (St Uny's) is signposted from the A3074 between St Ives and Lelant village. There is some space for parking near the church, and if you decide to start the walk at Carbis Bay there is a car park at the beach; but at both places parking is likely to be hard to find during the summer, and I would recommend using public transport, which by Cornish standards is very good in this area: trains on the St Ives - St Erth branch line are quite frequent (Lelant Station is perhaps a bit too far south of the church to be very convenient, but the one at Carbis Bay is ideally placed), and there is a "Hoppa" bus service that calls at Lelant Church, Carbis Bay and Halsetown: see current timetables.

LELANT

The ancient church of Lelant was the mother church of a very large parish until St Ives (1826), Towednack (1903) and eventually Carbis Bay (1948) were carved out of it. A Chapel of St Anta, a female member of the party who accompanied Fingar (see the note on Riviere, Walk 7), is said to have stood on rocks at the rivermouth ("Chapel Angier Point"), and the name Lelant is explained as a corruption of "Lananta", the form it took in the 12th century, meaning "church-site of Anta". The church itself, however, is dedicated to another member of that party, Uny or Euny, apparently one of the more widely-travelled of them, judging by the number of holy wells and churches that bear his name (Chapel Euny Well at Sancreed, and Redruth and Crowan parish churches, for example). It has been suggested that the centre of the old port is marked by the ancient "Abbey" house in what is now called Lower Lelant but was once Tredreath, the Town on the Sands; certainly the church now seems well away from the heart of the settlement, but foundations of houses have been found under what is now the golf course. ("There is a tradition," wrote Polsue in *Lake's Parochial History* [1870] "that a town of some magnitude, having a market and a custom-house, stood near the church, when the River Hayle afforded deep water without the aid of engineering skill, and before S. Ives had risen to importance.") Wind-blown sand has always been a threat on both sides of the Hayle River; it would appear from the early studies of Cornwall that the 16th century was a particularly difficult one from this point of view. John Norden's *Survey of Cornwall* (1584), for example, refers to "Uny-juxta-Lalant somtyme a haven towne, and of late decayde by reason of the sande which hath choaked the harbor, and buried muche of the Lande and howses; and manie devises they use to prevent the *obsorpation* of the churche." The most successful such "device", marram grass or "sea rush", was apparently first used in 1824. The church and its history are described in an unusually attractive and detailed guide, excellent value at 50p., so I'll just point out the pair of Norman pillars and the arch they support - much restored, but still a remarkable survival from the 12th or 13th century; the two delightful 17th-century slate memorials fixed to the wall near the font; and the lozenge-shaped Praed hatchment, hanging on the north wall. The Praed family, also commemorated in the lower of the slate memorials, lived at Trevethoe Manor and were the great landowners here as well as being very active "up-country": they were involved in the building of the Grand Junction Canal, and Praed Street in London is named after them. Outside, the Tyringham Vault, near the porch, commemorates the family who through marriage acquired Trevethoe from the Praeds. The churchyard is a good hunting-ground for old Cornish crosses. Of all the many Vicars, probably the one who left the greatest mark was Father R.F.Tyacke (Vicar 1869-1901), who arranged for the restoration of the church by J.D.Sedding after disastrous gales in 1872, and who founded the West Cornwall Golf Club.

1 From the main gate at Lelant (*) Church go along the road beside the cemetery, passing a chapel dedicated to Richard Perry in 1879. Continue beyond the West Cornwall Golf Club House for about a quarter of a mile.

2 Turn right where there is a sign announcing "Private Road to Rosewyn and the Links Holiday Flats Only". Watch for low-flying golf balls coming from your left: it might be wise not to pay too much attention yet to the view to your right, which already includes St Agnes Beacon and Carn Brea. Continue ahead on this entrance drive till you are almost at the house and flats, and go through the second of two small gates on your right. (Both bear warnings that you are entering private property, but in fact this seems to be the accepted route for walkers now that the public footpaths which traverse the golf course are unavailable, or at least inadvisable. I am grateful to John Nicholls of the Ramblers' Association, without whose *Six Coastal Walks with Inland Returns in Penwith,* Book 2, we would have been floundering about for a long time in search of the rights of way shown on the OS maps.) Walk down towards the sea beside the bank on the edge of the golf course; cross the gravelled path and continue for a few more yards to a wire fence, where you will find an obvious path running among gorse bushes to your left. Take this path, which runs above the St Ives Branch Line (*) and gives you fine views over Porth Kidney Sands and ahead to St Ives. ("Porth Kidney" apparently means "the pool of leave-taking" or "farewell pool", a name which invites imaginative explanations.)

THE ST IVES BRANCH LINE

Just over four miles long, the branch line from St Erth to St Ives was opened by the GWR in 1877. It was the last line ever built to Brunel's broad gauge; eleven years later it became what is known as "mixed gauge" when a third rail was added to enable standard gauge rolling stock to use it. The line played an important part in the development of St Ives as a seaside resort, just at the time when it was declining as a fishing port. Advertised by the GWR as its "Ocean Coast" line, the route has always been noted for its beauty. The two most impressive engineering works are both at Carbis Bay: the 78-ft.-high viaduct and the deep cutting. The rock here was so hard, it is said, that miners had to be employed to drive the cutting; "local legend has it that after finding lodes of the old Hawke's Point mine * they rather lost interest in railway matters, preferring to go prospecting". The quotation, along with most of the other information in this note, is taken from an as-yet-unpublished booklet about railways in this part of Cornwall, kindly sent to me by Mr Graham Thorne. From 1963 onwards the line carried passengers only, and the Lelant and Carbis Bay Stations were downgraded to halts; in 1971 St Ives Station itself was demolished to make way for a car park and what Mr Thorne calls "basic" facilities were provided in the former goods yard. A development that may have saved the line came in 1978 when the urgent need to reduce traffic congestion in St Ives led to the construction of a "park and ride" facility near the new station of St Ives Saltings.

* Hawke's Point Mine, otherwise known as Wheal Fanny Adela, was a small tin- and copper-producer that worked for several periods between 1806 and the 1880s. Adits (drainage shafts) open on to the beach below. Colourful details about the mine's history are given by Hamilton Jenkin in *Mines and Miners of Cornwall,* Vol. 1, and by Cyril Noall in *The St Ives Mining District.*

3 When you reach houses, continue past the first few and turn right on the downhill path which starts where a public footpath sign points back the way you have come. At the bottom turn right, cross the railway line with due caution, then turn left *(or take the coast path to the right if you want to return to Lelant now, picking up the directions at line 14 in point 10).* Keep left, ignoring the coast path sign. The narrow uphill path brings you to a footbridge over the deep railway cutting. From the bridge there is a fine view over Carbis Bay, with the "steeple" of Knill's Monument on the skyline. (The name "Carbis", by the way, derives from the Cornish "car-bons", a causeway or paved road; it is in fact the name of a farm that is or was situated close to the main road. An older name for the bay is Barrepta or Porthrepta.) Turn right at the T-junction on the path, and at the road turn right again.

4 *Now you have another opportunity to join the coast path back to Lelant: carry on over the railway bridge and look for the acorn sign on the right; pick up directions at point 10, line 2.* To continue the full walk, turn left uphill on the road past the St Uny and Boskerris Hotels. Immediately

WHEAL SPEED

This was the name of one of several ancient mines which were eventually amalgamated under the name of Providence Mines. "Carbisse, in St Ives" was mentioned as a tin mine in 1584, and Wheal Providence was working in the 1750s. By 1815 seven small mines had joined as the "United Mines", and these included Wheal Speed - one of those names, very common among Cornish mines, which imply a wish for good luck. The wish turned sour in 1821 when a dam burst in Wheal Speed. William Uren was drowned; his father, brother and a companion were rescued, but they had swallowed water mixed with gravel and were not expected to live. Five years later a miner died and another was badly injured when an explosive charge detonated too quickly. Providence Mines itself was formed in 1832 (Comfort, Grace and Good Fortune were among the other small mines involved) and became a large and profitable concern, "one of the great mines of this district", writes Cyril Noall, who gives a very detailed account of it in *The St Ives Mining District*. By 1869 one shaft had been sunk to 200 fathoms (1200 ft.), and in that year a man-engine was installed in another shaft to a depth of 150 fathoms for the benefit of the 300 men who worked underground. A vivid contemporary description of this man-engine is quoted by Cyril Noall (page 47). The mine closed in 1877 as a result of a slump in tin prices, and the last attempt to work it was from 1906 to 1916. A fine engine house from Wheal Speed survived till 1967 when it was demolished to make way for a housing estate - presumably the one this walk runs through.

beyond the latter, turn right and follow the public footpath signs. The pretty, wooded path runs uphill above the Carbis Valley and reaches the main road beside the St Margaret's Hotel. Cross with care and continue ahead on the path on the left side of the shop, C & C News. It runs beside a stream for a few yards, crosses a footbridge and brings you to a modern bungalow estate. Cross the road and continue ahead, still on a footpath at first, then along a road (Park Lowen). At the T-junction go right. This road, which curves uphill, is named after a mine called Wheal Speed (*). At the next T-junction turn left, then continue ahead past the "No through road" sign and Carminney Lane. Take the signed footpath to the right, which runs along the lower slopes of Warvas Hill, crowned by Knill's Monument (*). Many tempting little paths lead towards it, but every one we tried ended in a thick mass of the purple *ponticum* rhododendrons which must be a glorious sight in early summer but are looked on by conservationists as a menace because they tend to strangle all the native plants and are a poor habitat for wildlife. We were told that efforts are being made to open up at least one path to the top, but until that happens it's best to continue on the main path as far as the road. Bill Newby informs me that there are old mineshafts hidden among the vegetation, so pioneering expeditions could end in disaster.

5 There turn left. Near the top of the hill is a very clear sign to "Knill's Steeple", together with an attractive and informative notice. The breath-taking view from the Monument might, I guess, stretch as far as Hartland Point in exceptionally clear conditions, but the furthest coastal point we

KNILL'S MONUMENT

John Knill, who was Collector of Customs at St Ives and also Mayor of the town, became very wealthy partly through being a partner in a successful venture to recover treasure from a ship wrecked off the Lizard. He had the granite pyramid erected on Worvas Hill in 1782 as a mausoleum for himself which would also benefit others by acting as an aid to navigation. In 1797 he created a deed of trust by which he provided an annuity of £10 to pay for what Cyril Noall calls "a quaint little ceremony" to be held every fifth year. Ten young girls from St Ives, who must be daughters of sailors, fishermen or miners, have to dress in white, dance around the Monument for 15 minutes and then sing the 100th Psalm "to the fine old tune to which the same is sung in St Ives Church." See Noall's *The Story of St Ives* (Tor Mark Books) for further information and a photograph of the crowds that gathered for the event, I presume during the 1960s. Another lively account, which differs in some details, is given by David Mudd in *Cornwall & Scilly Peculiar.* "The saddest part of the story," says Mr Mudd, " is that he (Knill) does not lie buried in St Ives after all. Having made his elaborate plans, he left St Ives for a new post in London. While there, he became interested in medical research and left his body to a London hospital." Your next chance to witness the ceremony will be on 25th July 1996 ..... if this book is still in use after that, you'll have to make your own calculation!

could see was Trevose Head, near Padstow. The main landmarks working clockwise from there are Godrevy lighthouse, St Agnes Beacon, the huge waste tips of "china clay country", Carn Brea with a long range of hills to its right, then Godolphin and Tregonning Hills and Predannack Head on the Lizard coast. Further right and closer is Trencrom, with a glimpse of St Michael's Mount beside it, then Trink Hill, Rosewall Hill with mine stacks on its slopes, and finally St Ives. Return to the road and turn left - still uphill for a few yards, but then it runs down to Hendra Farm (the name actually means "Farm Farm", or more accurately "Home farm Farm"), which has been very well converted into a group of "studios" or small craft units.

6 Cross the wooden stile on the left - there is a footpath sign - and head for the houses. After crossing a stone stile, you walk along the right side of a caravan park (the Polmanter Farm Tourist Park, very nicely appointed with toilets, tennis courts, a swimming pool and a shop where I presume you could buy provisions during the season). Continue along the main entrance drive.

7 At the road turn right into Halsetown (*), passing a large converted chapel and several pretty terraced cottages. A big granite outcrop on the right matches the cairns and boulders on the hills above. The tall chimney on the skyline ahead is a relic of St Ives Wheal Allen, a tin mine which is said to have been working as early as 1730. Its main period of activity was during the 1860s. At the corner with the main road is the Halsetown Inn, a friendly "local" with a good name for food - a reputation which its new owners tell me they are determined to live up to. The pub's decor emphasises sporting interests (footbally, rugby, athletics...) but also has a selection of spoof adverts for drinks: Sheepdip Wine, Rum Bi-Carbi, Vladiawful Vodka, and

HALSETOWN

The name is pronounced "halls-town". It is a town only in the same sense as Lizard Town or Milltown, near Lostwithiel; compare the use of "churchtown" for the houses clustered around a parish church. Halsetown was built, or at least greatly enlarged, early in the 19th century by a Truro man, a mining entrepreneur who became MP for St Ives, James Halse (1769-1838). The obvious comparison, therefore, is really Charlestown, named after Charles Rashleigh. See also the comments on Canonstown, Walk 10. It seems like a pleasant place to live, thanks largely to the wide spacing of the houses, but the reason for that was less altruistic than you might guess, because, as Oliver Padel puts it in his *Cornish Place-Names,* "it is said that he planned this development in order to secure his parliamentary seat: each house had just enough land to qualify its tenant for the vote, and the tenants were his selected supporters." George Henwood wrote an essay during the 1850s about parliamentary reform and its effects on the mining industry around St Ives, painting a very favourable picture of Halse: see *Cornwall's Mines and Miners* (Barton, 1972). Arthur Mee's *Cornwall* states that "The great actor Sir Henry Irving lived here as a boy and found it a wild, weird place, full of fancies and legends." Halsetown Church - "enriched" as Mee says, with paintings by St Ives artists - is on the south-western edge of St Ives, about a mile north of the village. It was built in 1866 to a design by J. P. St Aubyn.

others less mentionable.

8 To start the walk back to Carbis Bay, return the same way, turning right immediately before the Post Office, where you will find steps down to a small path. Turn left on the track at the end, which runs beside some of James Halse's houses. One of them is a ruin, but the rest look lovingly maintained. Continue past a group of large modern farm buildings, then cross the stone stile ahead, where there is a public footpath sign. The path runs beside the hedge on your left, and after two more stiles and a couple of gates takes you down a few steps to a minor road.

9 Turn left on that. You are now close to the place where there was once a little village called Balnoon, "the mine on the downland": it was an ancient tin mine, revived during last century and the early years of this, and at some periods worked in conjunction with Worvas Downs Mine, whose sett covered the south-western slopes below Knill's Monument. The views of both coasts are scarcely less impressive than those from the Monument, which is quite close on the left; just after passing the picture-postcard cottage at Lower Varvas (another version of "Worvas") we noticed that the Goonhilly Downs Earth Station dishes were visible just to the left of Godolphin Hill. At the T-junction go straight on for a few yards, then follow the footpath sign directing you to the left side of the farm entrance drive. Beyond the farm buildings the path becomes a bridleway and heads towards Carn Brea and Hayle Sands, giving a particularly fine view as it starts going downhill. Soon after passing an old gipsy caravan (if it's stilll there), you are back on the route you came by, as described towards the end of point 4. Just in case you've forgotten which way you came: turn right (Wheal Speed Road), then second left (Park Lowen), and take the path which starts between Nos. 14

and 16 and runs beside the stream just above the main road. Cross that and continue on the path ahead, but this time instead of using the path you came on you could go straight on, thus walking on the other side of the Carbis Valley. It's a pretty walk, winding down beside the stream among attractive cottages and gardens, then past the White House Hotel (where refreshments are available, at least during the season) before passing under the viaduct. You emerge beside the Carbis Bay Hotel at the entrance to the beach, where there are toilets and beach shops. (Kenneth Brown tells me that sometimes at low tide greyish patches can be seen on this beach. They are caused by coal dust from the bunkers of three paddle tugs which were wrecked on the beach early this century. Being lighter than sand, the coal grains get washed to the surface.)

10 Turn right on the road. You now, I'm afraid, have a rather stiff climb to the point, near the top, where the coast path is signposted on your left. Just to add insult to injury, it starts by going quite steeply downhill! Notice the well-disguised World War 2 "pillbox" overlooking Carbis Bay. The headland is called Carrack Gladden, perhaps meaning "bank rock"; its local name, Hawke's Point, "properly belongs to the tiny promontory on its southern flank," says Cyril Noall. In *The Story of St Ives* he tells the legend of the Weeping Fern of Carrack Gladden: maidenhair fern used to grow profusely on the cliffs from here to Lelant Towans, watered by many tiny streams which left droplets on the fronds. The legend explains these as the tears of a girl who died of a broken heart when her lover drowned: her ghost weeps there still. Beyond the headland, keep to the upper path, which climbs quite steeply to rejoin for a few yards the path beside the railway line that you walked along earlier. Don't cross the line, but continue along the coast path, following the sign to the Nut Grove and Wishing Well. Unfortunately we missed the well, but I understand that it is only a short way along: after a steep downward slope the main path climbs again, but to find the well continue downhill for a few yards. To quote from J.Meyrick's *A Pilgrim's Guide to the Holy Wells of Cornwall,* it is "under a natural rock on the right and romantically situated in a nutgrove overlooking the sea. There is no building but the water is clear and it has a reputation as a Wishing Well which is its alternative name. It is also known as Fairy Well or Venton Euny." For your wish to be granted you have to drop a bent pin in the well as you make it, and you must keep the wish secret. The coast path continues among the twisted little hazels of the Nut Grove; looking ahead, it's quite hard to believe that the path actually runs along the steep cliffside: it's almost hidden by the windswept trees and shrubs that overarch it. Eventually you will emerge on to the dunes. This is another area that has been mined for tin and copper: early last century the mine was called West Wheal Towan; from 1850 to 1867, Lelant Wheal Towan; and in 1872 it was re-opened as West Wheal Lucy by the company that had recently started Wheal Lucy on the Phillack side: see Walk 7. West Wheal Lucy was even more short-lived than her sister. There are several points at which it's possible to cross over or under the railway and brave the golf balls and impatient gestures of golfers as you return to Lelant church, but it is more interesting to continue further along the shore. The odd-looking concrete structure just below the path on your left and the red-and-white box on stilts on the far side of the railway line a little further on house video cameras which enable the Harbourmaster at Hayle to keep a watch on the movements of vessels at the dangerous rivermouth. We were told, however, that the small black-and-white picture he receives is inadequate to show small boats. As you progress further south you have an excellent view of Norwaymen's Wharf (see the note in Walk 7) and of Hayle Harbour in general. Eventually the path brings you down to the beach at the point where a ferry was still operating when John Betjeman wrote his "Shell Guide" in the early 1960s. The most recent attempt to revive it was a short-lived one in 1981. Unless the tide is unusually high you can walk along the foreshore to Lelant Quay, an ancient wharf partially rebuilt during World War 2 when it was used by the Navy. Just before you reach it, notice how the sides of old ships - some of them complete with portholes and mooring cleats - have been used to prop up the sandy banks. These are a reminder of the scrap-metal firm of Thomas W. Ward Ltd, who used Hayle as a base for breaking up redundant ships, especially World War 1 destroyers, during the 1920s and '30s. (Martin Langley and Edwina Small have identified these remains as parts of a Torpedo Boat Destroyer, and they suggest "she may well be a veteran of Jutland." See *Lost Ships of the West Country,* 1988.) Somehow they seem to typify the appealing tattiness of so much of Hayle harbour in what may be the last of the Bad Old Days before the Golden Age of Peter de Savary finally dawns. If it ever does. In this context it's tempting to find symbolic significance in the iron skeleton of an old building which stands amongst the small derelict concrete structures - guard huts and such - on the Quay. We were told that it was taken over and used by the Navy during the war, and that in later years it was employed by Bickford Smith / ICI to store explosives for shipment. (Lelant Quay is commonly known locally as "Dynamite Quay".) There was once a railway siding to Lelant Quay, where the railway company had a steam crane, a weighbridge and warehouses, so it seems likely that the skeleton is a survival from that period. At the far end of the quay the path turns right and left before reaching a road across the golf course. The "bunkers" on the left side are a relic of the railway cutting to the Quay. From this road you have a good view of Hayle Hospital among trees on the hill above Carnsew Pool, and then the wide expanse of Lelant Saltings, a Mecca for bird-watchers. (Apart from the migrant waders and wintering wildfowl for which it is famous, we heard about kingfishers and a white egret which has been in residence for quite a while now.) Tropical birds can be seen nearby, too, along with eagles, penguins, otters, monkeys and more: Hayle's "Paradise Park" is on the hill slope below the hospital. At the far end of the Saltings is the ungainly bulk of the St Erth Creameries factory; the buildings by the shore near that are at another old wharf called Griggs Quay. Soon you will reach the "main" road near the church. Mrs Rosemary Balmer told us that Chygwidden ("white house") Cottage, where she lives, was once an alehouse, and that at that time - when the road to St Ives was no more than a muddy track - the larger house next door was the stables.

WALK 9

TOWEDNACK, AMALWHIDDEN AND ROSEWALL HILL

About 5 miles - or two walks, 1.5 and 3.5 miles

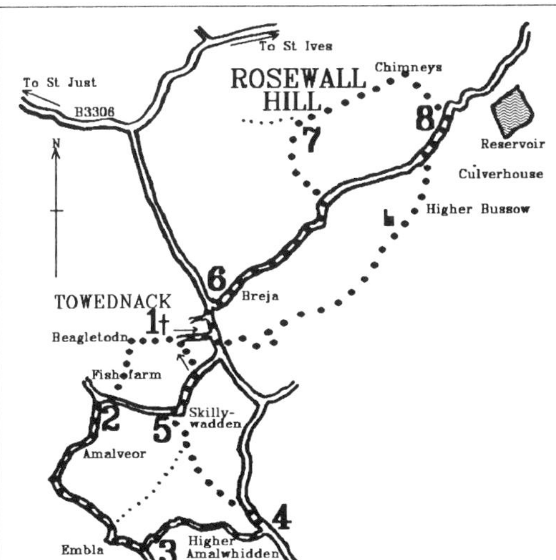

This is a figure-of-eight walk in true granite country - lonely, beautiful, and imbued with that special magic unique to West Penwith. It's out in the wilds, a long way from pubs and shops, so we took a picnic with us and left it in the car (parked at Towednack Church) while we did the short walk among places with intriguing names like Beagletodn, Amalwhidden and Skillywadden - just enough to give us a good appetite. We then embarked on the rather more strenuous walk up Rosewall Hill. Together they gave us a splendid day out. No doubt our enjoyment was enhanced by the fact that this was the first really summery day of 1992 - but I think we'd have found it rewarding even in driving rain, if we had been dressed for it: that would have shown us the other side of the coin of what living amid this landscape is truly like. As with nearly all the other walks in this book, the most important thing is to avoid misty conditions if possible, because the panoramic views are superb all the way - especially on Rosewall Hill, of course. (Another reason to shun the mists is mentioned below.) Towednack church is absolutely right for its setting, as the makers of the TV "Poldark" series in 1975 evidently recognised when they used it for funerals and weddings. The second part of the walk is particularly rich in mining remains. A few of the paths included on the routes are rather badly maintained: some climbing of awkward stiles, gates and fences is involved, and I would not recommend walking bare-legged, especially among the gorse-bushes that grow thickly near the top of Rosewall. Donald Rawe in "Cornish Villages" warns: "the explorer should avoid any possibility of being caught in the mist or inclement weather, for one may easily become pisky-led here."

There is plenty of parking space at Towednack church (*)- although as usual you should find an alternative when services are due. Towednack can be reached by taking minor roads from either the B3306 (St Ives to St Just road) or the B3311 (St Ives to Penzance): the roads are quite well signposted, but I'd advise consulting a map. The church car park is right beside the building, at the end of a narrow roadway.

TOWEDNACK CHURCH

This delightful little building was a mere chapelry of Lelant until the 15th century; even then it remained dependent on Lelant, not becoming a fully-fledged parish till 1903. Its independence was fairly short-lived, because since 1947 it has been linked with Zennor. These changes probably reflect the rise and fall of local population in parallel with the fortunes of the mines. The church is dedicated to St Tewennocus (hence the pronunciation "Twennock" for Towednack), probably an alias for St Winwaloe or Gunwalloe, who is the patron of St Winnow beside the River Fowey as well as of Gunwalloe on the Lizard. The sturdy little tower makes the church look as if it is huddled up in readiness for Atlantic gales; a legend tells that during the building of the tower the Devil came every night and demolished the part that had been added that day. At the south porch door, notice what look like very worn old crosses on either side and the interesting little sundial dated 1720 over the door; inside the porch a slab incised with a double cross is in use as a bench. One's first impressions on entering the building may be dominated by the work of the Victorian restorers (ceiling timbers brightly painted, the walls stripped of their plaster, once known for its pale blue colouring caused by a rare alga, and "snail-pointed"), but in fact much of historical interest has survived, including a chancel arch dating from about 1300 and an early altar of carved granite which was rescued from a wall at the farm close by.

THE SHORTER WALK, SOUTH OF THE CHURCH

1 Cross the granite cattle-grid/stile by the gate into the churchyard and go straight on, beside the hedge on your right. The hill fairly close on the right is Trendrine; further round to the right is Rosewall; Trink Hill is behind to the left, and in the distance to the left is Castle-an-Dinas: Rogers' Tower can just be glimpsed on the top. The farm ahead is Beagletodn, a name which Donald Rawe translates as "shepherd's grassland" but O.J.Padel explains as "warm navel" or "warm hillock". Cross two more stiles/grids and then turn left, with the hedge on your left now. Go through a wooden gate and then follow the white stones that lead you among the ponds and leats of a fish farm. The main business here is rearing trout, but one big pool on our left was populated by massive Koi carp. A stone footbridge takes you across a stream, and then a rather narrow path surrounded by brambles - quite likely to get overgrown later in the year, I guess - leads to a road.

2 Turn right on that. It curves left and goes uphill and gives you a view to the left of Knill's Monument and Trink Hill, with buildings associated with Giew Mine. The farm you soon pass is Amalveor ("great edge" or "great ridge"), where two gold bracelets, probably about three thousand years old, were found in 1931; next comes a house called Embla Vean ("vean" means small; "embla" has sometimes been explained as a plural of "amal", but Padel rejects this), and soon after that is Embla Farm. *(A footpath is signposted on the left shortly before Embla Farm. We did not use it, but we saw the other end of it, also signposted, and were told it is a clear and walkable path. I have shown it on the sketch-map. Using it would shorten the route slightly and enable you to avoid a rather overgrown path and a couple of partially-blocked stiles. Pick up the directions near the end of point 4.)* For the longer route, continue along the road a bit further.

3 Just before a bridge take the track on the left. It is used by horses and tractors and so tends to be muddy, and soon it becomes rather narrow and brambly. It widens again to a tractor track as it approaches Higher Amalwhidden ("white edge") Farm. The public footpath starting on the left just beyond the farm buildings seems to have vanished without trace, so continue down the farm entrance drive to the road.

4 Turn left there. Soon you reach Amalwhidden, where coarse fishing and holiday cottages are advertised. Immediately after the holiday cottages, cross the stile on your left, beside a rusty gate. Negotiating the stile was made as awkward as possible by strategically placed timbers and a length of rope, and the next stile was partially blocked in a similar way. I shall make enquiries about these and other problems with local paths, and hope to get some improvements made. The path runs beside the hedge on your right, beyond which is a lane which was formerly the right of way (the maps show it as such), but is badly overgrown after the first few hundred yards. There are five more stiles to cross, all of them unobstructed, and then you reach Skillywadden. I think I am glad no-one really knows what this name means. Oliver Padel suggests it may include the Cornish word "guan", weak, possibly as a nickname, but the "skilly" remains a complete puzzle.

5 At the road turn right, and after a few hundred yards cross the stile on your left (there is a footpath sign); the path runs by the hedge on your right at first, then curves left to a gate and the church.

THE LONGER WALK: ROSEWALL HILL

1 Walk along the church roadway and turn left at the end, passing the Old Vicarage and the entrance to Churchtown Farm. The farmhouse there was a pub about a hundred years ago, when the local mines provided plenty of thirsty customers.

6 Take the first turning right, past the converted barns of Breja (or Brega) Farm. The road runs uphill, and near the top, where there is a fairly sharp left corner, gives you a good view embracing Knill's Monument with Halsetown in the middle distance, Trink Hill with the Giew enginehouse very prominent, and Castle-an-Dinas crowned by Rogers' Tower. Some details about the nearby enginehouse are given later. A path should begin on the left hereabouts, but barbed wire made access difficult, so we went on a bit further to where the road curves gently right. At that point the fence was quite easy to cross. From there we backtracked a short way to the main hedge and walked beside that. It heads uphill, but a good way right of the top. Soon the path becomes quite a narrow one among gorse and heather and wanders further right, heading towards a cairn, and there are wire fences quite close on both sides. Just below the cairn we were faced by a barbed-wire fence across the path, but this was not too hard to cross at the right-hand end. (The name, Rosewall, by the way, seems to refer to a nearby ford, though I have not seen the ford identified: "the ford by the wall".)

7 At this point turn right for the main walk route. *You could first go left, towards the top of the hill, but be warned: another barbed-wire fence, a good deal harder to cross, bars the way a few yards from the boulder-strewn summit. Even so, you can get close enough to enjoy almost the full benefit of the magnificent view, apart from the coast to the west. It was a hazy day when we were there, but we could see Hayle Sands and Godrevy lighthouse, and in the south St Michael's Mount. George Henwood, writing in the 1850s, based an essay on the view from Rosewall Hill, arguing that it proves that the old phrase, "Fish, Tin and Copper" reverses the order of importance. See "Cornwall's Mines and Miners" (Barton, 1972). To make for the top, cross the rusty gate, held only by ropes at each end. The path goes a few yards right at first, then left, keeping just right of the low hedge or wall that runs up to the tor. This is the part of the walk where you're likely to suffer most if you ignored my warning about bare legs! To continue the walk, return the same way to the cairn mentioned earlier and continue ahead.* The path is fairly clear, running along the ridge. Notice the fenced mineshaft near the cairn, a relic of a tin mine called Rosewall Hill and Ransome United; many if not all of the smaller pits that pockmark the hilltop and upper slopes are the work of miners. "Many small but productive tin veins had been worked from ancient times" on the summit of Rosewall Hill, says Hamilton Jenkin, who also mentions that near the summit are the foundation walls of a round-house built to provide shelter for a horse-whim, where hoisting in a shaft was done by a pair of horses "which plodded round and round .... almost without attention, the boy driver sitting half-asleep on the capstan-bar." Go through the kissing gate. Soon a fine view over St Ives opens up, with two old minestacks on the slope just below, two ruined engine houses at the foot of the hill (pumping engine to the north, stamps to the south), and the Bussow reservoir in the middle distance. The mine buildings are more remains of Rosewall Hill and Ransome United, which is recorded as having produced a total of 1,500 tons of black tin at various periods between 1839 and 1876. Barton mentions that the workings were 200 fathoms (1,200ft) deep. Continue down to the lower chimney and turn right, beside a big fenced shaft. This path soon brings you down to the road.

BUSSOW CULVERHOUSE

This little building is probably 600-700 years old. Charles Henderson called it "the most interesting Columbarium in Cornwall" *(Essays in Cornish History).* Unlike many English dovecotes, which often contained about a thousand nest-holes, Cornish ones normally had about 250, and this one has just 156. The main opening for the birds is at the centre of the roof, but some Cornish dovecotes, including Bussow, also have a few holes in the walls for that purpose. The people in this area seem to have been unusually small when it was built, since the door is only about 3ft. high. The walls, which make no use of mortar, are some 50in. thick. Fledgling pigeons or "squabs" were a valuable source of fresh meat at a period when little besides salt beef and mutton was available in the winter: a breeding pair of pigeons could produce as many as fourteen in a year. The pigeons were used as baits in hawking, their eggs were eaten, and their droppings were good as manure. Dovecotes were probably introduced to Britain by the Normans, and until about 1500 the right to keep one was "restricted to manors and ecclesiastical fiefs" (R.D. Penhallurick). This one probably belonged to the manor of Ludgvan Leaze. To protect crops the dovecotes were usually sited on waste or common land distant from the manor house. For further information about culverhouses (the usual name for dovecotes in southern Britain) see Henderson's essay, Penhallurick's *The Birds of Cornwall and the Isles of Scilly* and *Some Aspects of the Domestic Archaeology of Cornwall* by Rosemary Robertson and Geoffrey Gilbert.

8 Turn right. Notice, among the fields to your left, a small round dovecot or culverhouse (*). After a few hundred yards, take the left turning with a "Private Road" sign, which leads to Higher Bussow Farm. The field on the left side of this path is shown on the OS maps to have remains of an ancient settlement of hut circles in it. (The name "Bussow" means "dwellings", but of course it may refer to comparatively modern ones.) Just past the farmhouse, cross the stile in the wall ahead. You are certainly very aware at this point that you are in granite country: such impressive boulders for a lawn-edging I've never seen! The track ahead leads to a ruined engine house which belonged to a mine called Tyringham Consols (*), but before you reach that cross another stile on the left, beside a farm gate. The path is clear, running across the field, through a gap, then over a stile to the right of the next gap. Beside it there is a yellow waymarker on a wooden post. From here on there is a succession of well-made stiles, mostly accompanied by yellow arrows, and the path runs fairly straight until you come to a fairly large field quite close to the church: here it follows the hedge on the left as it curves left and right before reaching the next stile, on the right of a wooden gate. One last stile brings you to the road, where you turn right and left to return to the church.

TYRINGHAM CONSOLS

An old tin mine called Bussow was reopened with this name in 1861, and the engine house was probably built then for a 40in. beam engine used for pumping. According to Hamilton Jenkin the mine met with little success and had closed before 1868. Two other authorities on Cornish mining, Collins and Dines, state that this mine was also known as West Wheal Providence, but Jenkin denies any connection. The Tyringham family, as mentioned in the note on Lelant church (Walk 8), became owners of Trevethoe Manor in succession to the Praeds; I presume they were the mineral lords at Bussow. "Consols", of course, is short for "Consolidated Mines", and the term had become associated with highly successful amalgamations like Fowey Consols, Par Consols, and the great Consols in Gwennap parish; Tyringham is one of many examples of very small enterprises that adopted the term, perhaps in the hope of luring potential adventurers.

WALK 10
TRENCROM

A round walk of a little more than a mile on the hill itself, with a possible "extra" of about 2 miles.

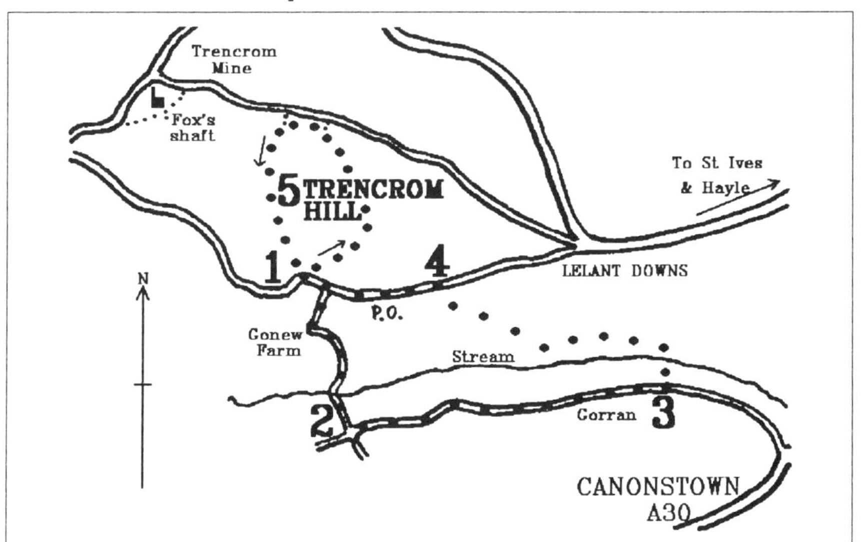

Trencrom Hill is a beautiful and historic place, and to stand on the summit on a clear day and study the view makes an ideal conclusion for the series of walks in this book. Little if any strenuous climbing is involved, because the start point itself is on high ground, but the path back down is steep in places, and I would advise you to wear shoes or boots with a good grip. The short extra walk I have suggested runs along both sides of a valley south of the hill and includes an old mining area. Most of the route is along well-made tracks or minor roads, but part of the path on the north side of the valley looks very likely to become overgrown in summer, and unless you have nettle-proof legs you would be wise to avoid wearing shorts on that section. On the other hand, we did get the impression that some clearing of the vegetation had been done shortly before we walked it in April 1992. A valuable companion for explorers of Trencrom is the National Trust's leaflet, with text by Professor Charles Thomas. If you don't already have a copy you will probably be able to buy one (only 20p in 1992) at the nearby Post Office, shown on the map. The longer walk route passes it. If you are particularly interested in natural history, I recommend "Wildlife Walkabouts: Land's End Peninsula, Cornwall " by Des Hannigan, which includes a walk on Trencrom.

There is a small car park, as well as room for five or six cars beside the road, on the south side of the hill, at the main entrance to the National Trust site. To drive there, take the minor road almost due west from Lelant Downs. The car park is on the right just before the road curves left as it approaches Ninnesbridge.

1 I'll start with the "extra" so that those who do it can save "the view from Trencrom" as a climax to the walk. (Incidentally, the full three-mile route is a figure-of-eight one, bringing you back to the car park before you climb the hill.) If you just want the short walk around and on Trencrom, start at line 4 in point 4. But for the valley walk, turn left on the road from the car park entrance, and then after a hundred yards or so take the wide track on your right. Ignore the left turn soon afterwards: keep to the downhill track as it winds past Gonew ("downs") Farm and among houses. In the valley-bottom are several pools beside the Canonstown Stream. (Canonstown, by the way, which is at the point where this stream meets the A30 about a mile east of here, is a planned village - compare Halsetown, Walk 8, and also Leedstown and Townshend in Crowan parish. The man responsible, John Rogers (1778-1856), was a canon of Exeter Cathedral.) Cross the footbridge beside the ford and continue ahead, uphill now.

2 At the T-junction turn left. This wide track is usually dry underfoot, apart from a couple of small muddy patches, and makes pleasant, fairly level walking. The hedges are quite high at first, but you get glimpses of Trencrom to the left and the sea ahead; later you have a clear view, including the attractive furzy little valley down to the left, dotted with old mineshafts on the far side. These are relics of Wheal Merth (*). Eventually the track becomes a tarmacked road serving the bungalows and new houses of Gorran. (The name of this hamlet presumably has no connection with the saint after whom the village near Mevagissey is named; perhaps, like Gonew, it derives from the Cornish "goon", downland.)

3 Where the road narrows, take the signed public footpath on the left, which goes down into the valley and crosses the stream by a footbridge. Ignore the paths on the left close to the bridge: go uphill, and then after 100 yards or so take the path, also on the left, which continues uphill among gorse and

WHEAL MERTH

This old tin mine was working at least as far back as the 18th century, and consisted of several small enterprises with colourful names such as Wheals Bag, Bucket and Strawberry. In 1849 it reopened with the name of East Wheal Margaret, probably in the hope that it would prove as rich as the Wheal Margaret which later became part of Wheal Sisters. (See Walk 2.) Hamilton Jenkin records that in 1862 it was employing 110 people, but three years later heavy losses forced the shareholders to sell up. Cyril Noall in *The St Ives Mining District,* Vol. 1, reproduces the auctioneer's announcement of items for sale, including "knives, forks, dinner set" from the Account House. Another attempt was made to work the mine, this time called Wheal Alice, for a few years in the 1870s; and it was active again under its old name of Wheal Merth from 1902 to 1907, employing some 30 people. Kenneth Brown tells me that the foundation can still be seen of the tandem compound horizontal pumping engine employed during this working. It was built at the Tuckingmill Foundry, and was also used at the famous Wheal Coates mine near Chapel Porth.

heather. Fork left soon afterwards. When you reach a wider path, go left on that. Notice the various fenced shafts in this area, as mentioned earlier. Go through the old wooden gate (lacking hinges when we were there), then walk along the left edge of the field. Don't go down into the valley. Just after you have passed the last of the bungalows at Gorran on the far side, go to the right where the field widens out, towards several farm gates. One of them has a rough wooden stile on its left; cross that. From here the path runs between hedges, and this is where nettles were making a take-over bid when we did this walk. Towards the end of the path a flimsy wire fence, easy to duck under, had been strung across the path - understandably, perhaps, since the right of way now passes through a cottage garden, uncomfortably close to the building. Continue ahead through the gate on the right to the road.

4 Turn left on that. Soon you will pass Flax Cottage, which rather surprisingly doubles as Lelant Downs Post Office, and the NT car park is not far beyond that.

For the walk on Trencrom itself I shall suggest a route which gives you a fairly gentle ascent and delays the arrival at the top till near the end; but you will see many other tempting paths, and I'd hate you to think I wanted to discourage you from exploring them! With that in mind, then, take the path on the right as you enter the car park, starting with a wooden barrier of the type known as a stagger gate. This path runs fairly level around the bottom

TRENCROM

The hill's name is taken from the nearby farm: *tre-an-crom,* farmstead of the curve, possibly referring to the circular hill-fort. The rampart is especially obvious on the west side (looking towards Carn Brea), but can in fact be traced all round the twin summits, and there are clear entrances, complete with gate jambs, on both east and west sides. The other gaps are probably of comparatively modern origin. You will have to look much more closely to see the remains of round houses, but archaeologists have counted the foundations of at least 14 (Craig Weatherhill refers to 16) within the enclosure. Stone axes dating from Neolithic times (c.3500 to 2500 BC) have been found on the hillside, and pottery of the period from about 200 BC to 900 AD indicates the other end of the time-span of human occupation here. Professor Thomas suggests that one advantage of sites like this in the Iron Age and Dark Age periods may have been that they offered safe enclosures for cattle and sheep when wolves roamed the woodlands below. Like Carn Brea, which has similar natural rock-formations on and around its summits, Trencrom has given birth to many legends of Giants and Druids; examples can be found in the 19th-century writings of William Bottrell and Robert Hunt, and several of them are outlined in Professor Thomas's leaflet. A plaque fixed to a rock at the top explains that Trencrom was given by Lt. Col. G. L. Tyringham (of Trevethoe: see the note on Lelant Church, Walk 8) to the National Trust in 1946 to act as a memorial to the people of Cornwall who died in both World Wars.

of the hill, curving gradually left for half a mile or so in all. Mrs Savill at the Post Office had told us to look out for a well, but we missed it; perhaps you will have more success. Bill Newby tells me that it is known as The Giant's Well and is on the left side of the path not far from the point where it first runs close to the road on the north side of the hill. Eventually you will pass another stagger gate, and then I suggest you follow the signed "horse track", which runs more-or-less parallel to the road; any muddy patches should be easy enough to step around. When the horse track gets close to the main entrance to the Trencrom site on the north side (where there is a house beside the road) it's finally time to head for the top. The path is clear.

5 Apart from the sheer beauty of the hilltop itself, with its natural granite outcrops, you will, I'm sure, notice the remains of the Iron Age hill fort: for some information about this and other matters, see the note on Trencrom. Inevitably, though, your main attention is likely to be drawn to the view, which extends much further than you might expect at a mere 550 feet above sea level. If you're a "local", or if you've done the other walks in this book, you probably won't need help with identification of the main landmarks - in which case, skip the next few lines. Starting at Godrevy Lighthouse and working clockwise: Hayle Sands; St Agnes Beacon in the distance; Lelant Saltings with Carn Brea in the background, and also possibly Brown Willy and Roughtor on Bodmin Moor; St Erth in the middle distance, and Canonstown further right, closer; Godolphin and Tregonning Hills; Predannack Head, not far from the Lizard; Perranuthnoe Church; St Michael's Mount; Ludgvan Church; Mousehole Island, Newlyn and Penzance; Castle-an-Dinas (the top of Rogers' Tower marks that, and the quarry on the left side); Trink Hill with an engine-house in the foreground; Rosewall Hill with mine stacks on its right-hand slope; and Knill's Monument, like a church steeple. The engine-house, a fine, ivy-covered one which is worth a closer look, belonged to Wheal Sisters, about which there is a note in Walk 2. It was on Michell's shaft in the Trencrom Mine part of the sett, and contained a 26in. rotative engine used for hoisting and pumping in Fox's shaft, which was further south on the Wheal Mary sett. (It is indicated by the word Shaft on the OS Pathfinder map on the south side of a short footpath: grid reference 513366.) A little to the right of the engine-house are the former count house (offices) and smithy of Trencrom Mine - both painted brilliant white in 1992.

To complete the walk, continue almost straight ahead, heading towards St Michael's Mount. Care is needed in some places, especially if rain has made the rocks slippery. The path goes to the right of the big round granite boulder which looks like a "logan" (pronounced "loggan"), and is known as The Rocking Stone. Soon you are back at the car park.

The Rocking Stone, Trencrom

LANDFALL WALKS BOOKS

OTHER VOLUMES IN THE SERIES

FOR MORE DELIGHTFUL WALKS NOT FAR FROM THE AREA COVERED BY THIS BOOK, SEE ESPECIALLY VOLUMES 4 AND 6.

No. 1 A VIEW FROM CARN MARTH, Seven Walks amid Cornwall's Industrial Past (1989) 52 pages, £2.50 (Now out of print)

No. 2 A VIEW FROM ST AGNES BEACON, Eight Walks amid Cornwall's Industrial Past (1989) 68 pages, £2.75

No. 3 AROUND THE FAL Circular Walks (1989, revised 1991) 62 pages, £2.95.

No. 4 AROUND THE HELFORD, Circular Walks (1989, reprinted with slight revisions 1990) 64 pages, £2.95

No. 5 AROUND NEWQUAY Circular Walks from Bedruthan to Holywell (1990) 64 pages, £2.70

No. 6 A VIEW FROM CARN BREA, Circular Walks around Redruth, Camborne and Portreath (1990) 80 pages, £2.95

No. 7 AROUND THE RIVER FOWEY, Circular Walks (1990, fully revised and reset 1992) 80 pages, £3.30.

No. 8 AROUND PADSTOW Circular Walks from Porthcothan to Wadebridge and Bodmin (1991) 68 pages, £3.30

No. 9 A SECOND VIEW FROM CARN MARTH 14 Round Walks near Truro, Falmouth and Redruth (1991) 144 pages including 26 colour photographs, £4.95

No. 10 AROUND ST AUSTELL Circular Walks from Pentewan to Par (1992) 68 pages including 10 colour photographs, £3.30.

No. 11 AROUND MEVAGISSEY Circular Walks from Portscatho to Pentewan (1992) 84 pages including 8 colour photographs, £3.30

OTHER BOOKS BY BOB ACTON

THE LANDFALL BOOK OF TRURO (1990) 16 pages, £1.25
Handy street-maps of Truro plus five round walks in and around the City.

THE LANDFALL BOOK OF THE POLDICE VALLEY
(1990) 72 pages including 8 in full colour, £3.99

ALL THE ABOVE BOOKS ARE AVAILABLE IN LOCAL SHOPS OR CAN BE ORDERED DIRECT FROM THE AUTHOR AT THE ADDRESS GIVEN ON PAGE 2.
Please add 50p per book towards postage and packing.
(This is based on 1992 postal costs.)